BEING & SWINE
THE END OF NATURE (AS WE KNEW IT)

FAHIM AMIR TRANSLATED BY
GEOFFREY C. HOWES
& CORVIN RUSSELL

Being and Swine
© 2020 Fahim Amir

Originally published in German in 2018 as
Schwein und Zeit: Tiere, Politik, Revolte
by Edition Nautilus, Hamburg, Germany. www.edition-nautilus.de

First published in English in 2020 by
Between the Lines
401 Richmond Street West, Studio 281
Toronto, Ontario M5V 3A8
Canada
1-800-718-7201
www.btlbooks.com

All rights reserved. No part of this publication may be photocopied, reproduced, stored in a retrieval system, or transmitted in any form or by any means, electronic, mechanical, recording, or otherwise, without the written permission of Between the Lines, or (for copying in Canada only) Access Copyright, 69 Yonge Street, Suite 1100, Toronto, ON M5E 1K3.

Every reasonable effort has been made to identify copyright holders. Between the Lines would be pleased to have any errors or omissions brought to its attention. Cataloguing in Publication information available from Library and Archives Canada.
ISBN 9781771134811

Cover by Caleb Mitchell
Designed by DEEVE
Printed in Canada

The translation of this work was supported by a grant from the Goethe-Institut in the framework of the "Books First" program.

We acknowledge for their financial support of our publishing activities: the Government of Canada; the Canada Council for the Arts; and the Government of Ontario through the Ontario Arts Council, the Ontario Book Publishers Tax Credit program, and Ontario Creates.

   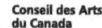 

"Free from typical boundaries of discipline or species, the freewheeling *Being and Swine* takes a novel jaunt through the history of thought and political philosophy: from Burke's scaremongering against the 'swinish multitude' unleashed by democracy, to Engels' famous struggle with the platypus, to the place of local pig-herding traditions in the development of the Frankfurt School. *Being and Swine* is filled with fertile polemics, witty detours, and swerves into burrows and sewers, pursuing unlikely bio-political insights that are sure to delight thinkers of any species."

JULES GLEESON, co-editor of *Transgender Marxism*

"Settle into *Being and Swine* and follow Fahim Amir through city parks, slaughterhouses, skyscrapers, military areas, supermarkets, construction sites, and many other places where humans and other-than-humans meet. From pigeon to platypus, from pigs to sparrows, honeybees to termites, engage with ecological and political imagination and know that nothing is untouched, nothing is passive. How is it that so many progressives miss the teeming, toiling, wily, freedom-seeking work of those political agents known as 'animals'? In this compelling, vibrant, and fascinating book, Amir offers answer and remedy as he describes animal actors, their acts of resistance to human power, and the lessons of such resistance."

CAROL J. ADAMS, author of *The Sexual Politics of Meat*

"Amir challenges us—especially those of us on the left—to acknowledge the behaviour of animals as inherently political. Woven through the social, political, and economic theory are refreshing and often amusing vignettes of collaboration between animals and humans to resist state and colonial authority, as well as animals acting in the independent pursuit of pleasure, rebellion, and revenge."

> **CATHARINE GRANT**, author of *The No-Nonsense Guide to Animal Rights*

"Amir's discussion of the challenges and possibilities of human-animal politics is not only thought-provoking, engaging, and wide-ranging, it is urgently needed. Social justice requires but also must move beyond *Homo sapiens*—and this has never been clearer."

> **DR. KENDRA COULTER**, Chair of the Department of Labour Studies at Brock University, Fellow of the Oxford Centre for Animal Ethics, and author of *Animals, Work, and the Promise of Interspecies Solidarity*

BEING & SWINE

For my father, Dr. B. Amir, poet and scholar

CONTENTS

- **xi** Preface to the English Edition
- **1** Introduction
- **23** Pigeon Politics
- **39** Swinish Multitudes
- **63** The Birth of the Factory
- **93** Underground Ecologies
- **121** Cloudy Swords
- **153** Black Hole Sun
- **175** Notes

PREFACE TO THE ENGLISH EDITION

Just two years ago I wrote in the original German edition of this book, *Schwein und Zeit*, that because of fear of the "swine flu," risk algorithms were dictating the occupational and social lives of people in the pork industry. Now, since the appearance of the novel coronavirus, people all over the world have had to adjust to biosecurity rules.

The fever of the COVID-19 disease was preceded, however, by the fever of the neoliberal reforms and free-trade agreements of the 1990s. The market radicalism associated with these reforms restrained government, which in many countries meant more poorly equipped public health care as well as a general reduction in government regulations in such sensitive sectors as food quality, livestock farming, and meat processing. The profit-driven exploitation of different standards of labour law and environmental protection was made incrementally easier. Thus, for example, the North American Free Trade Agreement of 1994 made it possible for US investors to set up industrialized hog farms in Mexico. Not long afterwards, in 2009, the "swine flu" emerged there.

In post-Maoist China, on the other hand, poultry farming was one of the first economic sectors to be opened to market mechanisms. But in the 1990s, major corporations pushed more and more small producers from the market. As a consequence, many farmers shifted to local species or unusual breeding lines. Among these were the wild geese that played a role in the "bird flu" outbreak of 2005. Similarly the rural poor were pushed to wild animals like bamboo rats, pangolins, or civet cats; the latter are considered the original hosts of the SARS outbreak of 2002–2003.

In many parts of Africa, the flesh of wild animals is called "bushmeat." Today bushmeat, which is associated with the occurrence of HIV and Ebola, is once again very much on the rise. Thanks to the roads that were originally built for mining and lumbering, hunters are pushing deeper and deeper into the forests. The increased hunting, consumption, and sale of bushmeat can in part be traced directly back to the collapse of small-scale fisheries. This was caused by industrial-scale overfishing by China, South Korea, and the European Union, and the ensuing collapse of fish populations along the African coasts. Moreover, the distinction between wild meat and conventional meat is less and less economically meaningful, since the wild-food sector is increasingly being formalized worldwide and is being capitalized by sources similar to those in industrial production.

All these processes and contexts drop out of view when, in media reports about a virus marked as "Chinese," attention is focused on seemingly extravagant culinary preferences and exotic "wet markets." At least the latter are public, while what goes on in Western slaughterhouses is usually withdrawn from public view. In the West, people like to invoke the local market and the small farm to illustrate contemporary ideas of the good and beautiful life. Within the self-righteous gaze on others, these ideas have rapidly transformed into the dystopian visual vocabulary of pandemic imaginations. To point out these sorts of connections between society, history, economy, everyday culture, and politics, without which neither nature nor the role of animals can be conceived, is one purpose of this book.

We live in a post-Chernobyl and post-Fukushima world. There is no going back. Still, we were not washed up totally alone, as urban flotsam the day after the party. If we look around us, we recognize the contours of other ecologies: virtuoso British songbirds full of synthetic hormones and Mexican bird nests full of nicotine undermine the idea of an "untouched" nature. Urban pigeons, as the "foreigners" of the urban animal world, adopt the city while the preservers of ecological order are exasperated by elderly women who refuse to be kept from feeding the pigeons.

Once the German dramatist Bertolt Brecht barked at his audience: "Don't stare so romantically!" Now we should also let our ideas of nature mutate. Criticism of environmental destruction is usually based on conservative ideas about "virgin nature," or it is transformed into ecocapitalist concern for sustainable resource management.

Being and Swine, however, is not about moral self-aggrandizement or market-based visions of social reform through correct consumption. It is about utopian impulses and animal revolts. Animals and humans are understood as members of the same political species. This can lead to non-innocent solidarity, instead of getting us stuck in the paternalistic traps of sympathetic ethics and the rhetoric of responsibility.

This shift of perspective to animals as political agents makes it possible to grasp their material and metaphorical significance in a different way. For example, animals no longer appear only as classist, sexist, or racist labels, but instead they prove themselves to be more-than-human discursive spaces within which struggles are articulated. This is another objective of this book, for animals not only share our (urban) spaces, they also inhabit our (political) dreams.

During an audience discussion after a reading from *Schwein und Zeit*, the director of a large residential facility for refugees reported that in the past few years it has not always been easy to explain "local" values to those who had fled from Lebanon, Afghanistan, and so on. There was only one thing she never wanted to hear about again: the refugees' persistent and incorrigible lack of understanding about why pigeons must not be fed.

Not only do most people today live in cities, this is also where the greatest economic output is produced, and where most consumption takes place. Therefore, the future of the planet will be decided in the cities. But neither nature nor the city is the same for everyone. For some beings, human and non-human, remaining in the public space is made difficult. Therefore, these connections cannot be separated from this question: Who does the city belong to? *Being and Swine* is also about this. One of its goals is to contribute to a broadening of the horizon of our political and ecological imaginations.

This cannot be done without humour, for the more politically charged a problem is, like today's "ecological crisis," the more crucial it is not to tense up when dealing with it. If you grab hold too hard, you might damage the object of interest, and what's more, not be able to let go.

Finally, a little reading advice. The chapters build on each other, but that doesn't mean at all that they have to be read in this order. Every chapter stands on its own and can be chosen according to the reader's own interests as a point of access to the book.

I cannot thank Arya Amir, Elke Auer, Alexandra Elbakyan, Alvaro Rodrigo Piña Otey, Katharina Picandet, Christoph Schachenhofer, Josefine Thom, Kerstin Weich, and Andros Zins-Browne enough. Without them, this book would not exist.

Fahim Amir, Vienna, September 2020

INTRODUCTION

Only a madman would say that animals are political. I am that madman. Maybe after reading this book, the idea of political animals won't seem so crazy anymore. But even if it does, that might not be so bad: as the German-American diva Marlene Dietrich once assured us, if you're not going crazy, you're not normal.

This already brings us to one of the certainties that this book raises doubts about: is the full possession of human mental (and physical) faculties an absolute prerequisite for being political, and if so, who does this leave out?

These questions can be traced back to the origins of the word "political," which derives from the ancient Greek *polis*: this was the term for the religious and administrative centre of the ancient city-state as well as for the collective citizens who assembled there. The site of the political was defined as a space to which neither animals nor plants, nor slaves, nor women had access. Here, only free Greek men were granted admission. All others were relegated to the margins of the *polis*, where they either had to work or got eaten up.

By contrast, this book pledges that resisting one's own domination is in itself genuinely political. This space of resistant politics is characterized by a continuum of forms of resistance, not by a winner-takes-all situation where on one hand, everything that is human is political, and on the other, everything that is not human is entirely devoid of the political.

Between the *resistant quality* of an animal bone against being processed and the full-blown *act of resistance* of a revolutionarily minded organization that has withstood trials by fire in numerous historical conflicts, there is a continuum of interconnected forms of acts of resistance and qualities of resistance. That animals are a part of this continuum is an essential concept in this book. This does not mean placing them on a par with humans, but it does mean working out "partial connections."[1]

An animal in revolt, of course, does not at all resemble conventional ideas of civic participation in civil processes of self-legislation. Animals don't draft petitions or start citizens' initiatives; they neither vote nor run for office. The French thinker Michel Foucault understood critique to mean refusal to be governed in some way. Who would deny animals the practical critique of prevailing conditions? Neither for humans nor for animals does critique have to be conceptual, conscious, or drawn up in civic terms; otherwise we'd be living in a world without countercultural fashions and styles, without the unconscious and dreams.

Instead of giving moralistic operating instructions from the judgment seat of ethics, that most bourgeois branch of philosophy, the present approach is conceived as a contribution to the formation of political solidarity. The ethical question "Can they suffer?" gives way here to this *political* question: where and how do animals put up resistance, and where and how have they done so? And subsequently, where have humans and animals been comrades-in-arms? These questions can produce a non-innocent solidarity that presupposes empathy instead of being limited to pity, which often bears the features of classism and chauvinism.

Even the first animal protection laws were steeped in class relations. One of the first animal welfare laws in the Western world, a British law for the protection of draft horses from insubordinate use of force by coachmen, shows this clearly. It was no coincidence that it dealt with the horse, which was regarded as "noble" and prestigious and needing protection from plebeian violence, while the legislators in the House of Lords had no problem hounding foxes to death in upper-class hunts. Another early animal protection law, likewise enacted in Great Britain, placed severe limits on dogfights. Cropping ears and docking tails to attain the appearance typical of a dog breed was not considered problematical, but gatherings of the emotionally stoked lower classes in unsupervised spaces very much was.

A glance at the present day shows the unbroken power of animal classism from above. The German reality series *Die Haustier-Nanny* (The Pet Nanny) is a contemporary case of such a class-based pedagogy that aims at the animal world in order to tame humans at the same time. An expert in pet husbandry visits families and their pets so she can "help" them. Every episode shows once again that these lower-class people not only dress tastelessly and live without style, but they also treat their animals badly.

Thus, animal politics—like every form of the political in capitalism—is always class politics as well. Since capitalism is always a neo-capitalism that ceaselessly revolutionizes its foundations and means, theory usually limps along behind real-world social changes. At the same time, we continue to live in capitalism, not post-capitalism, which is why staying alert to new developments and ideas is just as important as not losing sight of structural continuities. Additionally, we need to engage with cutting-edge scholarly discourses without letting Marxism get trimmed away.

Marxist analyses have been relegated to the margins of the academic world. In the face of headwinds, critical thinking tends to harden its position, to stiffen the defence of what has been realized, out of fear of losing even that—since current social reality offers little hope of a change in the weather.

Precisely in this situation, it would paradoxically be even more crucial to move ahead, to bring forward the most fitting and empowering ideas about the functioning of the present age and to gather the most committed forces in society around the most resolute analyses. Increasingly, some of these most committed forces are those concerned with animals. The aim of this book is to reflect on this positive development with analyses based in social theory and social history, and inspired by the most significant thinker on class relations. It is a contribution to critical philosophy—which Marx, as he expressed it in his letter of 1843 to Arnold Ruge, understood as the "self-clarification (critical philosophy) to be gained by the present time of its struggles and desires."[2]

WHEN IT COMES TO ANIMALS, THE LEFT TURNS RIGHT

The way East Germany dealt with the question of animals, as researched by Anett Laue in her book *Das sozialistische Tier* (The Socialist Animal),[3] could stand as an example of the predominant way the Marxist tradition has previously dealt with this question. It goes without saying that the total utilization of nature as a goal of socialist policy included animals as a part of that nature. The development of the broiler, that is, the industrial roasting chicken, was celebrated. Animal welfare groups were disbanded as an undesirable expression of the bourgeois individualism of "doggie daddies" and "cat ladies." This was not only "object-appropriate"—as the fitting treatment of animals was termed in state-socialist diction—but it could also invoke Marx. In the *Communist Manifesto*, Marx made a point of disavowing the "abolitionists of cruelty to animals," whom he counted as part of "conservative or bourgeois socialism" and who in his opinion were striving "to redress social grievances in order to secure the existence of bourgeois society."[4]

The East German state got its first animal-welfare law in October 1989, the last month of its existence. This law was the toughest animal-welfare law in German history, going far beyond the West German regulations, but it was too late: in reunited Germany, the vastly weaker West German animal-welfare law took precedence. The protection of nature fared better after the fall of the wall that divided capitalist West Germany from the "real existing socialism" of East Germany. The final resolution at the final session of the final East German government proclaimed that 4.5 percent of state territory would be placed under nature conservation. To this day, these areas are still protected.

What spurred this late change of attitude in East Germany was the strengthening of the environmental movement. Previously, the National Socialist Reich Animal Protection Act of 1933 had been in effect, with just two amendments, which eliminated the antisemitically motivated ban on *shechita* (kosher slaughter) and reduced the penalty for cruelty to animals from a maximum of two years to a maximum of six months.[5] Bruno Kiesler, director of the agricultural division of the Central Committee of the East German Communist Party, had already chided in 1962 that "we cannot be on the verge of achieving communism with an animal welfare law from 1933,"[6] the first year of Nazi rule.

Communism and fascism, united on the animal question? Even if this question seems provocative to some, since then we have made scant progress on a Marxist foundation. When it comes to animals, the left turns right. That means there is hardly any progressive positioning that is qualitatively distinct from the hegemony of bourgeois-liberal discourse. These times, however, demand it: if Marx made fun of the "sentimental societies for the prevention of cruelty to animals"[7] in a book review, US president George W. Bush was far from laughing when on November 27, 2006, he placed his signature under the Animal Enterprise Terrorism Act. This controversial law penalizes as terrorism any action aimed at damaging or interfering with the operations of an "animal enterprise." The title of a book that examines the consequences of this law for animal politics activists is telling: *Green Is the New Red*.[8]

ANIMALS—ANOTHER ONE OF THOSE PROBLEMS MARX DIDN'T SOLVE

Animals come up often in Marx's writings, usually to illustrate human labour or to specify its quality as distinct from "animalistic instinctive forms of work":

> We presuppose labor in a form that stamps it as exclusively human. A spider conducts operations that resemble those of a weaver, and a bee puts to shame many an architect in the construction of her cells. But what distinguishes the worst architect from the best of bees is this, that the architect raises his structure in imagination before he erects it in reality.[9]

When Marx imagines consciousness as an architect's brain, this bypasses the material praxis of architects and presents us with an *idealist* regression behind his own materialist insights. Works of architecture do not arise in the mind and then fall to the ground. The actual activity of architects is part of a larger topology of diverse forms of agency, of which functioning pencils and power supplies are just as much a part as unworkable building codes, unpredictable builders, and all kinds of surprises at the construction site—like mosquitoes and malaria.[10] The rational engineer/architect who outwits the witless bee in Marx's narrative is no chance example: the regulation of waterways and the erection of large-scale architectural projects were considered paradigmatic triumphs of controlling and harnessing nature in modernity.[11]

This implies two possible lines of inquiry for the Marxist confrontation with nature: Shouldn't current findings about the abilities and qualities of animals enter into reflections on Marxist thought? Marx prepared himself painstakingly for every article he published and read every source he could get his hands on. In this sense, new insights from ecology and ethology, philosophy, and economics could expand on Marx's fundamental assumptions without overhauling them structurally. What is Marxist in this line of inquiry is not the result but the method. This is how the US Marxist David Harvey thinks about the intentional goal-directedness of animals—that same intentionality that was important for Marx in human labour. We are, according to Harvey, also not the only organisms that transform outward nature and thereby transform themselves: "Ants do it, beavers do it, all kinds of organisms do it."[12]

The second line of inquiry argues that a reconstruction of fundamental Marxist categories is indispensable, as proposed, for instance, by the biologist and science theorist Donna Haraway.[13]

My perspective is an optimism of reason that tries to stay loyal to the first option as well as—in critical solidarity—to the Marxian project, especially by, among other things, integrating social-historical connections and bringing non-Marxian elements into a conversation with the Marxist classics. In my understanding, animals and animality are part of the continuity of *living labour-power*, which in the Marxist tradition is opposed to *dead labour*, another word for capital. The former can be tamed to a certain extent, but it can also become feral, a recurrent concern of this book.

The perspective developed here is not so much a Marxism intended as the foundation of a state, but the reanimation of an untamed and unpredictable Marxism. In this zombie Marxism, animals play a special role because they force us to rethink cherished aspects of theory, politics, and everyday culture.

VACATION IN THAILAND AND A NEW "TREND" AMONG CORPSES

At the end of the 1990s I wasn't yet twenty years old when I took part in a Buddhist retreat in Thailand, while my travelling companions hopped from one island to the next. Our group stay in Thailand had begun with a three-day island visit, so I was already familiar with that, and it held no charm for me. On the small ferry that brought us back to the mainland from our first stop, an official from the Thai tourist bureau happened to be riding with us. I used the opportunity to ask this friendly gentleman in a white shirt what Thailand tip he would give me if he could only make one recommendation. He didn't have to think long before suggesting I visit a particular Buddhist meditation centre. He told me it was actually intended for Thais, but for the first ten days of every month, all of the temple's offerings were in English so that foreigners could also get to know Buddhism. At this point, I had two follow-up questions. First, would there also be vegan food there? And second, how devout were the monks and nuns? That was to say, I had no desire for any more proselytizing after having just sat through ten years of Islamic, Protestant, and Catholic religion classes at school. In any case, this worry was groundless. At the meditation centre, which I actually did visit a short time later, Buddhism was imparted more like stoic philosophy or progressive psychoanalysis.

Once there, my food question was answered in the most wonderful way. Never again have I eaten such delicious Thai food as I did there. Except for two vegetarian meals during the ten days I spent there, the food was completely vegan. This couldn't be taken for granted: at the beginning of my vacation, in countless pubs and restaurants, at takeout stands and in bars, I had repeatedly tried to explain that I didn't want to consume any food made out of or taken from animals—because of language barriers, this mainly took the form of . . . pantomime. All you have to do is briefly consider how you would explain eggs, milk, and abstinence from them with gestures and facial expressions to imagine the amused faces of the Thais who witnessed these efforts.

This problem was solved in short order, again with the help of the Thai Tourism Office. A woman who worked there recommended that I should pretend to be a member of a Chinese sect that also existed in Thailand and was known for its vegan way of life. After all of those semi-public and admittedly somewhat unintentionally comical performances I had often found myself in, this was—despite its incompatibility with my worldview—an option definitely more agreeable than continuing to dabble in amateur acting on other continents.

From then on when I met people in Thailand who spoke little or no English, I passed myself off as a member of that sect (which, incidentally, in addition to animal products, had cut seven other foods like onions and garlic from its diet—I guess it was a package deal).

As I later realized, people will often more readily accept even the oddest food requests if the reason given for them is religious rather than ideological. In short, I made many new acquaintances and everywhere I went I was suddenly met with much respect and friendly interest as a person who by all appearances had travelled from the West and stalwartly stood by the culinary precepts of his Chinese sect, even on vacation. Before that trip I had erroneously believed that a vegan diet would not be a problem in Thailand.

Once there I was disabused of that notion. For example, I learned to my bewilderment that lately even the traditional coconut butter used in many dishes has one percent cow's milk added to it—in order to "refine" it. Even though this didn't change anything about the cooking qualities or the taste of the coconut butter, it did give it a sales advantage. It was almost as if its slight connection to cow's milk had allowed the common coconut butter to marry up into higher nutritional circles, or at least to be able to point to a distant aristocratic relative in its family tree.

Just to be safe, before the retreat began I had also inquired about this in the monastery that ran the meditation centre. There they assured me that they produce their own coconut butter, forgoing any additives. Because the monks were under a vow of silence, any further inquiries were forbidden as soon as the retreat had begun. "Retreat" meant a stay without any distractions like speaking, telephoning, or reading. It was intended to be an introduction to meditation techniques and the doctrine of Buddhism practised there. In the evening, we bathed in hot sulphur springs, segregated by gender, to regenerate ourselves, and we delighted in the nature romanticism of the swarms of bats that fluttered over our heads in the morning, returning from their forays (or whatever they were doing at night). All in all, a wonderful experience—even if the mosquitoes gave me trouble. Especially during the evening hours, they liked to land on the meditators. You could avoid this by applying mosquito repellent. I abstained from this, because it was most likely tested on animals, and I had neglected to look into non-animal-tested alternatives before I left. This was all the worse because meditation required peace and quiet, not an individual flailing his arms trying to chase away his personal swarm of mosquitoes.

Nor was my attempt to cover up with the few blankets I could lay my hands on, at least while meditating, crowned with success. As I might have imagined, the extra layer of textiles only led to increased body temperature, a more seductive lure for the tiny vampires to settle on my remaining unprotected body surfaces—in this case, my face. At the time, these conditions were not especially pleasant for me, but also not all that dramatic. Others might have had to struggle with back problems while meditating, or were not used to sitting on the floor for a long time.

What really shocked me didn't come until after the retreat. After getting familiar there with the classic variety of breathing meditation, we had the chance to learn about a form of meditation that is not very well known in the West: meditating in the presence of a decomposing corpse. The monks meditated for months while observing a human body as it gradually decayed. But this wasn't even the shocking thing. I was studying medicine at the time and was used to the sight of corpses. What was truly shocking was the fact that the monks in that back-to-nature monastery in central Thailand, which was located not far from the retreat compound in the middle of the forest (including howler monkeys in the trees and poisonous snakes by the waysides), had increasing difficulty obtaining corpses that would decay properly. More and more corpses didn't rot the way they have for millennia. Instead—especially, but not limited to, the ones that came from cities—they exhibited a strangely waxen skin. Most of the decomposition process was no longer really observable. This might actually be an advantage on aesthetic grounds, but the monks' explanation has stuck with me: they guessed that this new development had to do with the preservatives the dead had ingested via their food when they were alive.

EVERYTHING IS POISONED

These days, many people basically approach food in suspicion mode. Whereas unfamiliar food additives can at least be looked up, below a certain threshold, chemicals added during production don't even have to be listed on the food packaging. Additionally there are the largely unresearched interactions of many potent new molecules that find their way into the bodies of consumers every day. This is particularly true of animal products like meat, since substances ingested by way of animal feed can accumulate.

For many people, the mental and physical injuries inflicted on the animals are even more troubling than the harm they incur themselves. Probably everyone is against factory farming who has ever seen pictures of the conditions in such facilities. But what can be done?

As counter-images to the conditions of factory farming, we are usually subjected to romanticized visions of small farm production. The attractiveness of such historically backward-looking notions becomes clear when we think of how much they are used to advertise products that have nothing to do with them. Because the world back then still seemed to be in good order, idyllic scenes from this realm also function as screens onto which to project the idea of the good life in general. "In those days tomatoes still tasted like tomatoes." And you didn't have to worry about preservatives and carcinogens in your food. However, while in political theory it's usually only the conservative and reactionary forces that take their bearings from medieval conditions, for social theory about animals it is absolutely normal. But the world was not in good order, neither during the Middle Ages nor earlier. For example, the ancient Romans sewed the eyes of geese shut and nailed their pinions to the ground to fatten them up faster.

Although factory farming is a relatively new phenomenon, associated with capitalist means of production, this is not true of intensive livestock farming, which has been around considerably longer. "Small is beautiful" is no more automatically true than its opposite. But even apart from the many practices of premodern animal husbandry that seem abhorrent today, no pig has ever been petted to death on the farm, neither in premodern times nor in the "wellness capitalism" of the advertising industry. The violent killing of animals, involving fear, panic, and pain, is part and parcel of any small livestock operation. Organic marketing wants us to forget this for monetary reasons.

At the same time, it seems more and more people see traditional healing practices like Traditional Chinese Medicine (TCM) as a promising alternative to the products of the pharmaceutical industry and the methods of mainstream medicine (and its cruel animal testing). But because bear bile is an essential remedy in TCM, countless bear farms have been operating in China for some time now where the bears languish in long rows of cages that are so small that their arms and legs hang down between the bars. The sole purpose in life of these bears is their bile, which is continuously siphoned off from them. It's hardly surprising that traditional medicines for populations in the millions can only be produced by industrial means. At the beginning of the third Christian millennium, dark cyborg fantasies are a reality that seems to harmonize well with alternative lifestyles.

THE SAD ANIMAL MODERN

Looking at animals has fascinated people for ages. Today the entertainment value of animals often consists in their incomparably "authentic" performances of alienation and non-alienation. This is the real secret of the success of those notorious YouTube cat videos that are ubiquitous in contemporary popular culture. As a rule, the enjoyment of such visual meta-jokes about us human and non-human inhabitants of the modern world is innocent and harmless. It is a very different thing with the culturally pessimistic grief that is routinely involved in reflections on the changes in the human-animal relationship in modernity.

Thus the British art historian John Berger laments in his text "Why Look at Animals?" (1980)—which can stand as an example for many similar approaches—that the original "unity" that is supposed to have existed between humans and animals was disrupted by the imposition of capitalist forms of production and socialization.[14] Industrialization and urbanization, he suggests, have increasingly put space between animals and humans. Industrialization replaced horse power with horsepower, oxen with tractors, manure with chemicals, and so on. For him, "real" relationships between actual humans and animals have been increasingly replaced by visual and imaginary relationships—in the twentieth century, the culture industry eventually produced an explosion of animal representations. Never before in history has human culture been so heavily saturated by animal images in advertising, entertainment, and everyday culture. In this view, animals became a world of empty symbols that can inundate human society because real animals have vanished from human relationships. Nowadays, animals can stand for anything, because no one knows how real animals behave. Tigers sell cornflakes and purple cows peddle chocolate. So much, in a nutshell, for the position I call the sad animal modern.

The number of animal species exterminated, annihilated, and eradicated in the course of colonialism and capitalism is legion, and the miserable situation of animals in modern animal-processing industries, more or less like *the dead on leave**—doubtless a horror show of a leave—seems to confirm the outlook of the cultural pessimists. The inmates in animal factories look like frightful, pitiful caricatures of the relatively free fellow members of their species. In fact, the technoscientific practices of agriculture have spawned animals that seem like ghastly, grotesque ghosts of themselves.

What the critical proponents of the sad animal modern have overlooked is that the spatial separation in capitalist modernity between countryside and city, between production and consumption, has contributed decisively to a *debrutalization* of the human-animal relationship. While the slaughterhouses gradually disappeared from the cities, humans were able to grow up without the seemingly "natural" soundtrack of animals shrieking in fear on their way to the slaughter. What may appear to some as an overromanticizing of animals by the pampered souls of dangerously clueless city dwellers is for others the civilizing progress of the modern estrangement from customary barbarism. Only the spatial separation from the quaint, patriarchal brutality of rustic production made it possible to engage with animals differently than in the form of normalized violence and exploitation that calls itself a traditional "small farm." The same process that led to an immense quantitative increase and qualitative intensification of the exploitation of animals simul-

---

* As German revolutionary Eugen Leviné, upon being sentenced to death, famously referred to himself and his comrades.—Tr.

taneously brought forth its harshest critics and most implacable opponents.

Consider too how many migrants there are in modern societies. This does not mean there is a lot of interaction between these migrants and the majority society. Or think about all those misogynist philosophers who have stuck to their distorted convictions while knowing many "real" women from daily interactions. Neither for human beings nor for animals does spatial proximity automatically result in social proximity, or in particularly adequate knowledge of them. The chapter "Pigeon Politics" takes up this idea and traces an urban animal familiar to every modern city dweller, even if they have never seen any other "real" animal: the pigeon. It's possible there is more to learn from them than from the savviest cultural pessimist.

THE PERSPECTIVE OF STRUGGLE

This book is a plea for politicizing the animal question on the basis of a slightly "feralized" Marxism. This cause is urgent, because no matter whether hunting, zoos, circuses, or animal testing are at issue, no matter whether furs, foie gras, or factory farms are a problem, no matter whether whaling, animal transport, or even totally normal meat production is being criticized—few things excite hearts as much as animals do.

Yet instead of furnishing the most progressive forces for social change with more probing and far-reaching answers that go beyond the promises of liberalism, Marxist approaches plod along behind them.[15] In both its analysis of the role of animals in capitalism and its critique of the status quo of animals in specific societies, the left often recalls a sad, perplexed rearguard.

This is even more true of the Marxism that, when it comes to animals, has never emancipated itself from bourgeois liberal discourses—if it even ever had anything progressive to say about the topic that went beyond naively Hegelified or idealist-humanist platitudes. What Paul B. Preciado says about feminism also applies to the history of the workers' movement. Voices from within this movement were at first marginalized and then forgotten, so that they now appear "weird." Hence the point here is to reflect on a few central foundations of the political debate around animals and give a different account of them from a Marxist perspective.

If for a moment we put aside those hopeless Marxists for whom socialism consists in the utterly perfected domination and exploitation of animals, and ignore ultrahumanists who refuse to speak about animals as long as all human problems have not yet been solved for all time, most people would probably agree that animals ought to be protected from undue or extreme violence. This political front is marked mainly by two differing approaches: first, animal welfare wants to gradually improve the lot of animals; and second, animal rights activists and animal liberationists aim to abolish ownership of animals.

But regardless of whether they are animal welfare or animal rights activists—one thing unites both sides on this front line: animals are thought of as passive victims of the woes of the world. Contemporary moral philosophies also occupy this

Archimedean point when they regard animals as dependent "moral patients" as opposed to autonomous humans as "moral agents"; this position was also taken by the critical theorists Theodor W. Adorno and Max Horkheimer in their *Dialectic of Enlightenment* (1947), where they described the treatment of animals as an essential aspect of the inward and outward domination of nature.

Here these positions on the animal question will be confronted with another viewpoint: thinking the history and presence of animals *from the perspective of struggle*. If, as is often said, Marx stood Hegel's dialectic on its (idealist) head in order to gain a (materialist) footing, that still doesn't go far enough—this footing must include hooves and paws as well. The whole apparatus of fences, cages, pens, and surveillance and monitoring systems is an answer to the monstrous agency of animals and a testament to their world-forming power, as opposed to the usual thinking about them in terms of deficit (too little linguistic competence, too little capacity for abstraction, too little ability to plan, and so on).

I propose conceiving of animals as political agents of resistance and understanding animal resistance as a motor for modernizing capitalist forms of production. Here, animals will be thought of not as half as intelligent, or a quarter as creative, as humans, as popular science likes to do, nor as being secondary entities without their own quality of existence, but as powerful co-producers of world.

ENGELS APOLOGIZES TO THE PLATYPUS

In a letter of March 12, 1895, Friedrich Engels reports on his apology to the platypus, that wondrous creature that more or less straddles two biological orders—a mammal that lays eggs. The letter was addressed to the economist and philosopher Conrad Schmidt (who was also the older brother of the sculptor Käthe Kollwitz).[16] In this letter, Engels argues that concepts are approximations of reality. This does not reduce them to a mere arbitrary fiction, but they must not be simply equated with reality.

By way of illustration, Engels mentions two examples. One comes from social history, and the other from natural history. Medieval feudalism surely never existed anywhere in the world in "full classicism," that is, immaculate in terms of economic theory—what came closest to the theoretical system were the surviving legal texts of the short-lived Kingdom of Jerusalem.

Engels's second example, to which he devotes twice as much space as to feudalism, concerns the tension between models that classify living beings into rigid taxonomies (like fish, amphibians, or mammals) and the nimble dynamics of life in its continuous evolutionary transformation:

> From the moment when we accept the theory of evolution, all our concepts of organic life correspond only approximately to reality. Otherwise there would be no change: on the day when concept and reality in the organic world match absolutely, development is

at an end. The concept "fish" implies a life in water and breathing with gills; how do you want to get from fish to amphibian without breaking through this concept? And it has been broken through, and we know a whole array of fish who have evolved their air bladder into lungs and can breathe air. How do you want to get from the egg-laying reptile to the mammal that bears live offspring without bringing one or the other concept into conflict with reality? And in actuality we have in the monotremes a whole subclass of egg-laying mammals—I saw the eggs of the platypus in Manchester in 1843 and in haughty close-mindedness I mocked the foolishness of it, as if a mammal could lay eggs, and now it's proved! So don't do to the concept of value the same, on account of which I had to beg the platypus for forgiveness![17]

Maybe it's time for more critical minds to follow Engels's lead and start apologizing to animals for "haughty close-mindedness." The walls of that old *polis* fell long ago.

PIGEON POLITICS

We must be wily like the pigeons.
—Toni Negri

On June 22, 1966, an article appeared in the *New York Times* that was to make (pigeon) history. In it, Thomas P. Hoving, the city's parks commissioner, harshly condemned the vandalizing and defiling of Bryant Park. Hoving explicitly singled out "homosexuals," who he said were "pulling faces" at other park patrons, and pointed out the extraordinary number of "winos" congregating in the green spaces. The article described a public park in crisis, hopelessly overrun by homeless people and shamelessly misused as a garbage dump. This was followed by a subheading: "And then there are the pigeons." Hoving declared this heretofore blameless bird species to be New York's "most persistent vandal . . . the pigeon eats our ivy, our grass, our flowers and is a health threat. . . . But everyone seems to want to feed them. . . . It's impossible to stop the pigeon-feeders."

After the author's appeal—more desperate than hopeful—for a "clean-up," at the end of the article a phrase appeared for the first time that was destined to follow pigeons everywhere they went: "Commissioner Hoving called the pigeon 'a rat with wings.'" Woody Allen's 1980 film *Stardust Memories* quoted this New York expression, vaulting it into global circulation.[1]

In no time, the public image of pigeons was transformed. Once the epitome of the delicious, the beautiful, the wholesome, and the good, in the course of the twentieth century they were increasingly viewed in more and more Western cities as an urban plague: nasty, ugly, and germ-infested.[2] But how did this transformation come about?

One important material reason for the high esteem these birds enjoyed was likely their ability to produce what is perhaps the world's best fertilizer: pigeon droppings have been valued by agrarian societies across time and space. In the most remote corners of the globe, dovecotes and pigeon towers stand as monuments to this esteem. Generally regarded as peaceful, monogamous, and handsome, pigeons—in this context called "doves"*—became the symbol of the Holy Spirit in Christian mythology, which for its part could draw on existing traditions of dove veneration. In Catholic lore they were considered the only creatures on earth so pure that no demon could ever possess them. Doves are among the earliest domesticated animals and they have accompanied human societies since there have been written records. Homer, Socrates, and Aristotle exhibit quite an intimate knowledge of how doves live, and they wrote

---

* The German word *Taube*, which is cognate with the English word "dove," is used for both the wild dove and the domesticated pigeon and its feral urban descendants.—Tr.

about their selective breeding and domestication. Visual, sculptural, and literary depictions of the relationship between humans and doves go back five thousand years. Some authors trace their domestication to the beginning of sedentary societies in and around the Near East and North Africa ten thousand years ago.

All domesticated and urban pigeons are descended from the rock dove, which still exists today. But while its urban descendants are found almost everywhere there are humans, the rock dove occurs only in Asia and Africa. The pigeon is regarded as what is called a synanthrope, or companion species. Interacting with humans and their buildings has proved to be highly advantageous for pigeons. It appears that the earthen and stone structures of the first human dwellings resembled the original habitat of pigeons so much that they were readily commandeered as nesting sites. Pigeons, that is, do not build nests; they set up accommodations in existing nooks and crannies. And since pigeons hardly seemed to care about the difference between nature and culture, they got comfortable around humans and showed little fear of them.

These traits peculiar to pigeons were the prerequisite for human interventions. Their rapid reproduction cycles made them ideal breeding stock; Charles Darwin himself devoted many years to observing them. Pigeons, it turns out, are fertile longer and more often than most other animals. Thus they became mythical beasts in various cultures, standing for gentleness and monogamy, for fertility, and for the good as such. No wonder that doves were popular sacrificial animals and temple birds, consecrated first to Aphrodite and later to

Venus. According to Pliny, the ancient Romans developed a regular obsession for dove flesh and ate them as nestlings after force-feeding them with half-chewed bread and getting them prematurely fat. Just one of the many Roman dove towers could house five thousand doves.

Even in the seventeenth century, around 26,000 dovecotes still existed in Great Britain. Only in the eighteenth century did their numbers drop considerably, as the introduction of root crops allowed large livestock to be fed even in winter, significantly reducing the demand for dove flesh.

In France, erecting a dovecote was a privilege of the uppermost social classes. It wasn't just the old order that fell in 1789, but all dovecotes as well. Today it is estimated that a third of all pigeons in France are traceable to the doves that were liberated in the course of the French Revolution. During the siege of Paris in 1870–1871, messenger pigeons flew 150,000 official messages and about a million private ones over the military fortifications.

FLYING MOLES

Although their function as messengers was gradually displaced during the nineteenth century by technological innovations, pigeons remained eminently important in Europe until the turn of the twentieth century as an inexpensive source of food and fertilizer, and as natural weedkillers.

The development of the Haber-Bosch process at the beginning of the twentieth century transformed traditional agriculture and shook the material basis of dove worship. Since nitrogen was the most important factor for increasing agricultural production, its successful synthesis had far-reaching economic and social consequences, including a rapid decline in the importance of pigeon droppings. The rise of the chicken as a comparable source of nutrition, which started in the United States in the first half of the twentieth century, took further wind out of the pigeon's sails. As it turns out, the chicken keeps laying eggs even under immense bodily and psychic stress and highly industrialized farming conditions, and tries desperately to stay alive when other species would long have given up the ghost.

In this way, the postwar economic miracle transformed the mythical image of *Schlaraffenland*.* No more roast pigeons flying into open mouths. Around the turn of the century, about 750,000 pigeons a year were eaten in Vienna alone, but in the course of the twentieth century this number sank to zero. Within modernized agriculture, there was no longer any economically productive place for pigeons in the highly industrialized regions of the world. The disappearance of horses from the public space

---

* *Schlaraffenland,* literally "land of lazy apes," is a medieval fantasy land of plenty still widely known to German audiences from the Grimms' repackaging of the story in their compendium of German fairy tales. In it there is the image of roast pigeons flying into the mouths of the land's lazy inhabitants; the expression "waiting until roast pigeons fly into your mouth" has become proverbial in German for expecting something without working for it. Parallel images involving geese and larks exist in the medieval Anglo-Irish Land of Cockaigne.—Tr.

also meant a significant reduction in food sources for pigeons, which had been in the habit of feasting on horse feed scattered on the street. There was one exception, in mass culture, to this loss of an economic role: pigeon breeding. Especially among the miners in the Ruhr region of Germany, up to 100,000 pigeon fanciers busied themselves part-time every day with keeping, breeding, and sport—well into the twentieth century. It was a part of proletarian leisure culture when those who dug for a living below ground affectionately called them "flying moles":

> Training, discipline, and work on the clock are what the miner himself has to accomplish, and what he also demands of his beloved pigeons. He disciplines his soulbird just as he has to discipline himself. What he experiences in pigeon breeding, and in the flight of the birds, as his own liberation consists, among other things, in bringing his own constraints as a dowry to his union with the pigeons: the realm of freedom he creates reflects all of these constraints, not only as their mirror image transfigured into goodness—it contains them in bodily form.[3]

MILITARIZING THE FACADE

The same economic processes that increasingly tarnished the dove's halo also led to an explosion in pigeon populations in the world's urban zones. The Fordist postwar boom bestowed on them an increased food supply in the form of litter, and the advent of shopping streets and pedestrian zones provided them with an abundance of natural/artificial habitat. As they had done in the earliest human settlements, pigeons also made themselves at home in the new metropolises and took possession of the city. After losing their erstwhile economic value for human beings in the course of the twentieth century, their status changed appreciably too. Halved and laid on a wound or eaten in a soup, for example, the dove was long considered healthful, ideal nourishment for the sick or hospitalized. Well into the 1950s, dove was a weekly fixture on the menu in half of Vienna's hospitals, a bird thought to be so pure that it would even heal the sick. But increasingly it was perceived as a disease carrier.

Home interiors grew more and more aseptic, and city exteriors ever more groomed. Higher standards of hygiene made private individuals worry about the cleanliness of their window ledges and backyards. Businesspeople and local politicians fretted about the aesthetics of public shopping areas. And although any squirrel spreads more pathogens than pigeons do, the latter came to be seen as "germ factories." That people are so ready to believe this points to a symbolic urban order in which visions of disciplined city spaces merge with commercial demands for sanitized zones of consumption at the intersection of orderly aesthetics and biosocial hygiene. In such spaces, not only pigeons, but other figures perceived as parasitical and useless—punks, beggars, junkies, graffiti artists, the homeless—become disturbers of the tamed cityscape and the regular flow of business.

Even if the German Federal Supreme Court has ruled that pigeons are definitively not pests, building cleaners and similar stakeholders with an interest in cleansing the city of pigeons still like to claim that they are. Consequently, in the fight against pigeons facades have been militarized with spikes and nets. Pest exterminators are ready to assist. Eco-moralistic signs in parks showing rats wearing nasty scowls pull off a semiotic short circuit to another pest whose status seems unambiguous: feed a pigeon and you feed a rat.[4]

THE VISUAL ECOLOGY OF DIRT

The sociologist Colin Jerolmack combed the archives of the *New York Times* for the period from 1851 to 2006, looking for evidence of the demonization of pigeons as a problem species. He comes to this conclusion: "I contend that pigeons have come to represent the antithesis of the ideal metropolis, which is orderly and sanitized, with nature subdued and compartmentalized. While typified as a health issue, the pigeon's primary 'offense' is that it 'pollutes' habitats dedicated for human use."[5]

Dirt, as the anthropologist Mary Douglas has shown, is primarily a social category.[6] Dirt does not exist as such. What looks like dirt under a goldsmith's fingernails, once removed and put in the right place, is pure gold. Or, as an old British saw has it, "Dirt is matter out of place." Applied to living beings, this means: the attribute "dirty" denotes subjects that are to be removed from a certain space.

This is the secret of the increasing public antipathy towards pigeons. It's *not* because they're dirty that pigeons should be removed from urban spaces; it's because they disturb the new urban order that they appear dirty.

Their visibility is part of the problem. In contrast to badgers, polecats, deer, and other denizens of the borderlands of nature and culture, pigeons are not found on the periphery of cities, but they live in the most public, most visible places in the city. In contrast to rats and cockroaches, they do not emerge only at nightfall, but exist within the city in the bright light of day. They can fly away, and have always done so, which is why they cannot be banished indoors like cats or put on a leash like dogs.

The pigeon also runs contrary to another constant of domestication: since most domesticated animals no longer have to find their own food, they are intellectually inferior to their wild counterparts—with pigeons, it's the other way around. Contrary to the philosopher Jacques Rousseau's fears, it appears that civilization does not always lead to ruin. Pigeons in general occupy a middle zone between domesticated and wild animals, because urban pigeons are the feral descendants of once-domesticated animals, which also often bred with their wild cousins from outside the city. From the perspective of urban ecology, city pigeons are viewed as a "bastardized" population of individuals that did not duly return to their dovecotes or, as happened in France after 1789, were freed from them and joined the feral fellow members of their species: city air brings freedom, apparently sometimes to non-humans as well.*

ON POISONING PIGEONS

In postwar Austria, the pigeon briefly assumed a role that was special in many ways. In the tabloid media, stories appeared that presented pigeons as both victims and villains:

> Representatives of the Vienna Animal Welfare Association have been working as detectives the past few weeks, and what they have finally turned up is scandalous: Vienna's pigeons are being taken in large shipments to Bologna. . . . Just yesterday, another pigeon shipment left Vienna's South Station, bound for Italy. Five hundred pigeons in six small crates set off on the four-day trip to Bologna. There was hardly any feed or water in those crates.[7]

In its outrage over the fate of the abducted pigeons, Austria the good was able to stand tall. But even at that time,

---

* The German proverb *Stadtluft macht frei*—city air brings freedom—refers to a principle of medieval law by which a person in feudal bondage who made it to a city and lived there for a year and a day was then bound to the city and free from their former obligations.—Tr.

the contours of today's pigeon problem were already showing themselves. And a Viennese solution for it was already in place:

> Each year in Vienna, approximately 15,000 pigeons are to be exterminated. The City of Vienna commissioned a pest-control company in the Landstrasse district to perform this controversial but sadly necessary task. The men of this company are proceeding according to a carefully established plan for decimating the pigeons where they have become a serious nuisance. This involves scattering corn kernels treated with hydrogen cyanide. As soon as the creatures swallow a single kernel, they fall over dead. The Animal Welfare Society cannot intervene against this form of pigeon extermination because it is totally painless and humane.

Thus, the claim that hydrogen cyanide is a particularly humane form of eradication also contributed to relativizing the cruelty of Nazi crimes. The final twist came through reporting on how other capital cities were dealing with the now-vexatious birds:

> Moscow declares war on pigeons. . . . After the medical school at the University of Moscow blamed the city's constantly expanding flocks of pigeons for influenza epidemics, millions of those cooing birds are to be banished from the Soviet metropolis. . . . With gigantic vacuum cleaners, the pigeons will

be sucked up from the streets and Red Square and resettled in Siberia.[8]

In postwar Austria, people thought that the ultimate terror—which some still felt in their bones—was being a prisoner of war in Siberia. The reporting on pigeons, with its monstrous promises (humanity through cyanide) and improbable premises (obliteration from the face of the earth through vacuum cleaners) reinforced its own logic of justification. The violence and hypocrisy it contained shortly after the eradication of one of the most important centres of Jewish life in Europe by the National Socialists must also have struck the anarchist composer and poet Georg Kreisler when he returned in 1955 to Austria from the US, where he had fled from Nazi terror. No wonder that his perhaps most famous song, "Taubenvergiften im Park" (Poisoning Pigeons in the Park), was banned from radio and television.

FEED A PIGEON, FEED RESISTANCE

The philosopher Jacques Derrida devoted his final lecture to the bestiality and wolfishness of sovereignty, setting it against non-violence and dovishness.[9] In this case, the otherwise astute thinker of deconstruction was taken in by the hegemonic history of ideas, and overlooked the dialectic of olive branch and fecal bomb.

Unlike English, the German language does not know the duplication of *Taube* into "dove" and "pigeon." The conceptual Gemini constellation of good doves and evil pigeons, however, must have at least seemed familiar, for it recalls the gendered pair "virgin" and "whore." Let's not kid ourselves: the two names mark legitimate and illegitimate movement in public space. The careful parcelling of the two forms of *Columbidae*, which are genetically and zoologically indistinguishable, shows the influence of social technologies: the white dove of peace, meekness, monogamy, and obedience belongs to ceremonies of state, peace accords, and weddings.

The pigeon became the outcast of urban wildlife, whose aggressive guano threatens to corrode national cultural monuments, and who doesn't belong anywhere. It conforms neither to conventional notions of wild beauty nor to the husbandry of servile livestock. That is why pigeons are to be the targets of recent species-appropriate prosecution—preferably in "ecological" form, with falcons that are virtually officers in the service of municipal administrations.

Yet pigeon numbers are declining, because gentrification crosses even species boundaries. The increasing use of glass for building exteriors and the continual upgrading of attics into penthouses are reducing the nesting sites and sheltering spaces available to pigeons. Added to this are the effects of deterrent measures like nets and spikes. Bans on feeding pigeons are also slowly showing some success, and undeveloped urban spaces are disappearing.[10]

Michel Foucault once defined critique as "the art of not being governed or, better, the art of not being governed like that and at that cost."[11] In this sense, pigeons emerge as unruly creatures. On the basis of their numbers, visibility, and tenacity, pigeons assume a special role as disruptors of the urban order.[12]

In humans too, such recalcitrance both affectively and viscerally resembles old folks' dirty jokes more than a deadly serious petition drive.

In the urban space, we find a human figure associated with pigeons: the elderly person, or more precisely, the elderly woman. Like animals, older people are also thought of as a home for conservatism and inflexibility. Thus, in the typical urban imagination, two losers meet in public spaces: the haggard grandma who squanders her excess affection on something that does not seem worthy of it; and the object of that affection, the pigeon. But what if feeding pigeons reveals contours of a large-scale affective militancy among older people in the public space? When as "granarchists" they pursue their publicly condemned practice of feeding the pigeons, old women really do take on joggers, park wardens, and the like.[13]

The pigeon is a living metaphor for excess and communication, for insubordinate migration without a fatherland, and for producing solidarity in improbable places. The pigeon is a cipher for wealth, proliferation, and sociality ("pigeons fly to where pigeons are"). It is based in material, non-innocent history and the associated multifarious production of meaning. But the pigeon is also just as much a sign of excess and of the utopian: in *Mary Poppins* (1964), the children break loose—instead of taking their savings to the bank, as their father demands, they give it to the old beggar woman who sits on the steps of St. Paul's Cathedral, selling pigeon feed.

Interestingly, pigeons became a problem of urban pollution just when portions of the left wing discovered dirt for themselves. If the right to cleanliness, that is, to adequate opportunities for washing and bathing, was a self-evident demand of socialist and communist groups until the mid-twentieth century, now beatniks and punks emerged as movements in popular culture that related positively to dirt. The punk with a rat on his shoulder or a mutt on a leash has become a familiar figure. As far as human-animal relations in urban ecology go, however, the punk remains within the bourgeois framework of property ownership. He's merely switched animals. Thus the relationship between older women and pigeons, who can come and go as they please and belong to no one but themselves, can be seen as a social-revolutionary praxis. To paraphrase Foucault, we can say: Where there are cities, there are also pigeons. And where there are pigeons, there is resistance.

SWINISH MULTITUDES

> If biopower symbolically equated animals with poor men,
> the workers' reaction was not to negate the equation, but to
> creatively turn it into a struggle for life.
> —Nádia Farage

Pigs were an ordinary part of preindustrial cityscapes in Europe and elsewhere, where they were seen on streets and squares—but that doesn't mean everyone was happy about it. By 1410 German cities like Ulm were already making efforts to limit the number of pigs per inhabitant and tried to reduce the time a pig was allowed to run freely around the city (one hour at midday). For a long time, these efforts were not crowned with success. In Berlin, raising pigs was banned, and in 1709 the Hamburg Senate resorted to posting placards to inform the public about the odours and health problems caused by pigs cavorting unimpeded around Hamburg.[1]

At some point, more precisely, the first half of the nineteenth century, the grunting denizens of New York became the subject of a fervent debate when gentrification and class resentments, pigs and police, affluent citizens and less affluent migrants of Irish, English, and African-American descent, and men and women clashed both verbally and physically over the issues of the free movement of pigs in public spaces and the importance of the city as a common good. This encompassed proposed legislation and street fights, letters to the editor and petitions, and disinformation campaigns and demobilization attempts.

It was a time in which migration and class relations were rearranging the urban topology of New York. The city was growing enormously, which suddenly shifted neighbourhoods that were once spatially and socially far apart into immediate proximity, along with their class-specific ways of life. Even under Dutch rule in the seventeenth century, various ordinances were aimed at regulating the nuisance caused by free-roaming pigs, but for the most part they were ignored.[2] In more troubled economic times, such as after the War of 1812, the number of pigs rose sharply, since this was a way poorer classes could easily earn extra income: the pigs could not only be eaten but also sold to local butchers. Compared to other livestock, keeping pigs also required a minimum of work: in the urban environment, pigs autonomously foraged for their own food and trotted home in the evening of their own accord. These forays were eminently successful, and even important for keeping the city clean. At that time guaranteeing the cleanliness of the sidewalks, for example, depended on private initiative, and was not considered a function of the municipal government.[3] The result was that in poorer quarters, where there were almost no servants to clean up in front of the buildings, lots of trash piled up. The pigs reduced this refuse and thus paradoxically made the less affluent zones of the city cleaner. The pigs were "the city's shame, but nevertheless, its only efficient scavengers."[4]

When in the years after the War of 1812 the number of pigs in New York grew to approximately 20,000 (with a total human population of about 100,000), pressure mounted from better-situated circles to run the pigs out of Manhattan.[5] The morals, eyes, and noses of the cultivated crowd were visibly irritated. New York had become one big "pigsty."

Abijah Hammond, one of the wealthiest landowners and merchants in the city, succeeded in 1816 in getting two hundred prosperous pig opponents to sign a petition demanding the removal of all free-running pigs. After repeated delays, the proposed ordinance was put to a vote the following year, but without winning a majority. The reason for this lay in the resistance of swinekeepers, who, as news of the proposal spread, quickly assembled under the leadership of the African-American street sweeper Adam Marshall. Within two days Marshall had managed to get eighty-seven people, including women and illiterate supporters, to sign a counter-petition.

Their counterarguments: with such a law, the poor would no longer have anything to eat in the winter, and the streets would be buried in filth. This mainly convinced the city councilmen from the poorer quarters, who couldn't refute these points and were afraid of losing the confidence of their constituents. The proposed law was quashed.

This process would be repeated twice, in the form of petitions and counter-petitions, proposed laws, and revised decisions. Neither side spared the other: while the anti-pig faction made fun of a Black street sweeper leading women and illiterates, Marshall's group retorted that informants were infiltrating their neighbourhoods and stealing swine for their own use. Marshall prevailed, and the pigs went on knocking over elegant ladies and stirring up a ruckus in the streets.

In 1818, in the midst of these conflicts, a new mayor's term had begun. This was Cadwallader D. Colden, who refused to accept the stalemate between pig opponents and pig proponents. Colden, who came from one of the oldest and most established New York families, had been appointed by the governor and therefore cared much less than the elected city councilmen about balancing the interests of various groups in the city. Besides, he had no need to fear being voted out of office anytime soon. To realize his dream of a pig-free city, he banked on a strategy of mastering the situation by prosecuting specific individual cases.

In the same year, an opportunity presented itself: a butcher named Christian Harriet was accused of neglecting his duty to supervise his pigs, thereby causing a public nuisance. Harriet decided to defend himself and engaged a lawyer. Now a proper judicial trial could be scheduled to serve as an example:

> Van Wyck, the district attorney, began the case by examining a Mr. Ames, Harriet's neighbor and evidently another pig keeper, who reluctantly admitted that Harriet's hogs had been seen in the streets.... A series of horror stories was produced to show the evil of pigs in the streets, for example: (1) hogs attacked children, (2) boys got into trouble by riding

hogs, (3) ladies had been compelled to view swine copulating in open view, and (4) hogs defecated on people. The defense called no witnesses.[6]

Under pressure from the mayor, Harriet was ultimately convicted of inciting a public nuisance. The continuing stream of complaints and letters to the editor in the following years, however, showed that this strategy of convicting individuals according to the precedent of *The People v. Harriet* was not particularly successful as a general deterrent.

Two arguments against the free-running pigs of New York were advanced especially often. First, it was frequently objected that the sight of the pigs made an unfavourable impression on visitors to New York. This was no doubt accurate, but many visitors turned out to be more generous than expected, when in humorous deprecation they identified the pigs with all Americans and their passion for pork.

Another argument often advanced was that the pigs knocked down well-dressed women and landed their clothes in the mud. From a feminist point of view, of course, this was a questionable argument, since many of these pigs belonged to women living on their own whose very survival—not just the temporary tidiness of their garments—would be threatened by the ban on keeping swine.

It did help mobilize men who saw themselves as gallant heroes—the semi-feral domesticated pigs had become modern dragons and vanquishing them was a challenge to the knights of New York.

In her book *Taming Manhattan* (2014), Catherine McNeur

argues that this campaign against pigs involved class resentments from above that were directed just as much at those unruly quarters with their Irish, Black, and immigrant occupants—among them "unseemly" women. This is especially evident in the many caricatures and lampooning verses, letters, and columns in newspapers, where the pigs and their keepers, their qualities deemed interchangeable, were made into laughingstock.[7]

HOG RIOTS

In 1821, the next mayor, Stephen Allen, tried again. Allen's strategy was to order any free-ranging pig to be captured and immediately transferred to the poorhouse, where it was to be prepared at once as food for the inmates. Allen's ulterior motive was to quell criticism of the war against pigs, which was also a war against the needy, by feeding the pigs to the poorest of the poor. But this strategy foundered too: the hog catchers met with bitter resistance from hundreds of pig owners, their pigs, and whole neighbourhoods who made a stand against the kidnapping of their animals: "Locals assaulted the hog catchers with mud, rotten food, hot water, and broomsticks. A riot had begun. The rioters were a diverse group of women and men, largely made up of working-class Irish and African-Americans."[8]

In response, the city council suspended the ordinance in the districts of the city where the resistance was especially strong. But these "hog riots," as they were called, kept happening. In 1825, 1826, 1830, and 1832, the city was rocked by numerous uprisings that usually played out according to a similar pattern: whenever a wagon had been loaded with confiscated pigs, a cry went up for their release, while more and more people from the neighbourhood gathered on the scene. If the demand was not met, hundreds of residents would block the streets and sometimes attack the hog catchers and the police escorting them, opening the wagons and freeing the pigs, who quickly scattered in all directions.[9]

Angry neighbours and squealing pigs put whole neighbourhoods in an uproar. The fortitude of the residents against the responding officers and the flouting of the law amazed even the newspapers: "Moreover, after the 1830 riot, one newspaper complained that all of the people attacking the hogcarts, as well as those involved in another riot a few days later were immigrants who seemed not to understand the system of American law."[10]

Thomas F. De Voe, an eyewitness to several hog riots, reports on a typical pig melee in 1825, "where the . . . hogcatchers, and also the officers who attended them, were either cheated out of their prey, or obliged entirely to desist, . . . [and] almost every woman, to a man, was joined together for common protection in resisting their favorites from becoming public property."[11] The complaints of wealthy New Yorkers persisted, but the pigs, their owners, and the neighbourhoods that protected them had won the day and would continue to do so in the many swine rebellions over the following years.

Only an outbreak of cholera in 1832 gave the city administration and the supposedly well-meaning citizens the pretext they needed. Although the cholera had nothing to do with pigs, the cholera panic was so great that the hog catchers and their police escorts were finally successful in hunting down the hogs. Thousands of hogs were "pignapped." The fear that the cholera would return paralyzed the city for the next two decades, while complaints about hogs marauding in the streets gradually abated, as did the number of unruly swine. It took until 1849 for the streets of the "more developed" areas of New York to be totally swine-free. What laws, the pressure of public opinion, police, and hog catchers could not achieve came about with the help of a cholera epidemic of which the pigs were totally innocent. Medical horror stories had ultimately proved to be the mightiest ideological weapon of "sanitary despotism"[12] for demobilizing the swinish multitude.

For that is how the assemblage of resistant humans and pigs were referred to over and over again on the streets and in literally hundreds of articles and letters to the editor: as a "swinish multitude."[13] In this expression, disobedient humans and animals were unified as a collective power of resistance.

PLEBS & PORK

The expression had been coined several decades before by Edmund Burke, a precursor of political conservatism, in his 1790 diatribe against the rebellious masses of the French Revolution, *Reflections on the Revolution in France*,[14] and later it became so popular that it found its way into the hog battles of New York. Borrowing wording from the Gospel of Matthew,[15] Burke had warned that the French rabble would let pigs trample all that was valuable in human civilization:

> Nothing is more certain, than that our manners, our civilization, and all the good things which are connected with manners and with civilization, have, in this European world of ours, depended for ages upon two principles; and were indeed the result of both combined; I mean the spirit of a gentleman, and the spirit of religion. . . . [But now], along with its natural protectors, and guardians, learning will be cast into the mire, and trodden down under the hoofs of a swinish multitude.[16]

Carl Fisher understands Burke's image of the insolent swine as "anxiety about the disruptive potential of social insubordination and unruly demotic politics."[17] For Burke, the social-revolutionary forces of the French Revolution threatened the natural order. This new world would only invert the relationships between men and women, and between upper and lower classes, in a terrible way (a topsy-turvy world, like free-running hogs). The pig was a destabilizing image: "For the conservative, the 'swinish multitude' epitomizes the threat of democracy and the need to keep the populace in check; for the radical, the phrase exemplifies aristocratic discrediting tactics and fuels the desire to reciprocate in kind."[18]

Although Burke was perhaps ill-advised in his choice of words—after all, the expression became a target for pretty much every progressive thinker and author of the time, from Mary Wollstonecraft to Thomas Paine, and led to the founding of a periodical that published poems in favour of the French Revolution and was titled *Swinish Multitude*—he does correctly describe the interpenetration of emotional, physical, and cognitive dimensions in that "unruly crowd," like those insurrectionists who stormed the Bastille and marched on Versailles, and went on to execute the French king and the Habsburg princess at his side.

Burke's talk of the swinish multitude was both a surrogate and a harbinger of something that was not yet discernable in the spume of history, because it was only beginning to rise out of the sea of social-historical antagonisms: the proletariat. The swinish multitude in Burke is a monstrous figure, because the monster disrupts both the natural and the social order that spawns it.

What is monstrous in the swinish multitude is characterized by both mobility and lawlessness, because the swinish multitude abandons the order of things. Its monstrosity for Burke is as much a warning as an omen, in keeping with the original meaning of the Latin word "monster."* It is Burke's name for that which is unnameable, since "the French Revolution saw him faced with a new collective entity only beginning to emerge on the historical stage—a 'mobbish' multitude which would later become the proletariat."[19]

---

* The *Oxford English Dictionary* gives the classical Latin etymon of "monster" as *mōnstrum*, with "portent" among its meanings, based on *monēre*, "to warn."—Tr.

THE COMMUNIST MANIFESTO AND
THE SMITHFIELD MARKET

Stephen Eisenman notes that Burke's words are not merely more or less successful metaphors, but that they bear within them the echo of the hurly-burly, the plebeian and pre-proletarian bustle of the Smithfield Market.[20] The more usual term for the working classes at this time was "giddy multitude" or "vulgar multitude." "Both had been in use from the days of the Stuarts, rehearsed during the time of the English Civil War, and repeated ever since."[21]

Significantly, Burke used this term to express the idea that rebellions and revolts in his times consisted not only of people who behaved like swine (as in France), but also of pigs and other animals that behaved like people. The real swinish multitude was a term for the riotous chaos of humans and animals, for political radicalism in troubled times of social conflict. According to Eisenman, the Smithfield Market in the London of the 1790s might have provided the real inspiration for Burke's coinage: "For more than a decade, an incipient war was waged between elite Englishmen and domesticated bulls, pigs, and sheep, with some radicals joining on the side of the latter."[22]

Since the number of animals traded here had multiplied twentyfold in less than a century, without any new space having been provided for them, "on market days—Mondays and Fridays—it was an ear riot of animals, vehicles, tradesmen, prostitutes, hawkers, mountebanks, beggars, ruffians, and cutpurses."[23] Dead animals were lying around, while others were being goaded with whips—often to the point of panic. In the eighteenth century, the expression "an over-driven ox from Smithfield Market" became a byword for someone who had been "provoked to the breaking point."[24] Many times, individual animals or whole groups of animals turned against the drovers and trampled them. Indeed, stories of enraged and rampaging animals were widespread in the newspapers of the time. Bull-baiting, or "bullock hunting," even made a plebeian sport out of it.

Eisenman quotes a report in the *London Chronicle* from 1798 about bullock hunters as "professed thieves":

> They make choice of the wildest bullock in a drove, and then enrage the animal by every possible means, till he quits the herd in pursuit of one of the gang. Being singled out, they bid defiance to the drovers and owners, and run him for many hours, exciting the attention of the public, while the hunters steal everything they can get at. They terrify the people, and carry off their booty.[25]

Especially in the 1790s, this violent and disruptive folk tradition occasioned exhaustive newspaper reports, which expressed not only general concern about these potentially seditious situations, but also devoted much column space to fears of the erosion of work discipline as well as the waste or even destruction of labour power.

While these rebellious and riotous people were ritualizing something that had always existed (animals that flipped out, broke out, and ran away), the bullock hunt also occasionally took on the guise of a criminal enterprise: onlookers shouted from the sidewalks or tried to escape to safety, all while gang members moved calmly through the hubbub, picking objects of value from the pockets of the distracted. Sometimes the plebeian blood sport or the criminal enterprise (or both at once) about an animal "breaking out" became reality, and the getaway succeeded: "In this setting they might either be terribly abused or enabled to vent their rage and seek liberty."[26]

The livestock market was a site of fraying bodies and tempers in times of political unrest:

> But concern with rampant animals and bullock hunting was about politics as much as public safety. The spectacle of bulls, goaded by ruffians, running rampant down Oxford Street or the Strand, destroying property, and tossing pedestrians was the veritable image of social chaos—the world upside down—feared by anti-Jacobin Tory and Whig alike.[27]

Eisenman refuses to see this as merely a metaphor:

> To argue that aggression like this is merely instinctual or autonomic in animals while comparable violence is purposeful or political in humans is to understate the cognitive depth (or self-consciousness) of the first and overstate it in the second. In fact, autonomic and somatic systems work in conjunction. Animals confined, abused, or who are about to be killed emit fear pheromones detectable

by other animals through vomeronasal organs, found at the base of their nasal cavities. These threatened animals in turn produce stress hormones that trigger the classic and recognizable signs of fear: rapid breathing and heart rate, sweating, loud vocalizations, agitated movements, and physical aggression such as that demonstrated by the rampant animals at Smithfield. These reactions, which we sometimes describe as fight or flight, also have a cognitive dimension. . . . Most large animals, to put it simply, know when they are glad and when they are angry.[28]

When Burke thus refers in his *Reflections on the Revolution in France* to the radicalized masses as a "swinish multitude," he might have been closer to the mark than he is generally given credit for. Grief and affection, occasion and opportunity, along with large numbers, are the driving forces behind social protest. Marx and Engels write in the *Communist Manifesto*: "But with the development of industry the proletariat not only increases in number; it becomes concentrated in greater masses, its strength grows, and it feels that strength more."[29] For Eisenman this is "as much a biological as a social observation, and it may be applied to working or domesticated animals as well as to humans."[30]

Interestingly, the greatest number of injuries from bullock hunts coincided precisely with the period of the greatest fears among the elites about the repercussions of the French Revolution and the rise of English radicalism. At the same time, in socially critical paintings such as *Promis'd Horrors of the*

French Invasion, or Forcible Reasons for Negociating a Regicide Peace (1796) by James Gillray, raging bulls are depicted as part of scenarios of urban revolt—previously, pigs in paintings had stood for flourishing landscapes, personal wealth, and secure property (often including a particularly well-nourished specimen).

THE SITUATION OF WORKING PIGS IN ENGLAND

In the context of the working class, the pig was not only part of a subsistence economy that made workers less dependent on the vagaries of the labour market and the economy, but also an expression of the wretched conditions they lived in. In his report on *The Condition of the Working Class in England*, Friedrich Engels points out that one of the peculiarities of the areas he describes was "the multitude of pigs walking about in all the alleys, rooting into the offal heaps, or kept imprisoned in small pens."[31] The dwellings of the Irish population looked to Engels like "literal piggery* . . . repeated at every twenty paces," with swines "wandering unrestrained through the neighbourhood."[32]

In general it was assumed that workers keeping swine would lead to criminality, since it was not possible for them to legally feed pigs in cities. For the sake of their pigs, workers would be forced to turn to crime. Mark Neocleous therefore concludes:

---

* The German *Schweinerei*, "piggery," also means "mess."—Tr.

> It is not too much of an exaggeration to say, that the pig was, in effect, part of the working class. The pig has therefore been at the heart of class politics. The closeness of the pig to the Worker encouraged the ruling class view that the line between the "respectable working class" and the "criminal class" was impossible to draw. . . . For the ruling class, then, the pig was a problem for all sorts of reasons: it created the possibility of a Worker having some sort of subsistence without the wage, it was an indicator of slum conditions, it led to bad hygiene, it was symbolic of an absence of civilised life, and it generated a propensity to commit crimes against property. More than anything, the closeness of the pig to its urban working class owner appeared to the Bourgeoisie as evidence of the Worker's own swinishness.[33]

After Edmund Burke's "rebranding" of pigs as part of the revolutionary masses, republican and radical factions were positively disposed toward pigs. In poems and songs, pamphlets, and even on tankards, the rebellious masses were represented either as pigs themselves, or in the company of pigs. In Brighton Museum in England a beer tankard made in the 1790s is on display that shows Burke giving a speech to some pigs. In one hand he holds a paper on which "Thoughts on French Revolution" is written. From his mouth comes a speech bubble containing a rhyme: "Ye pigs who never went to college, You must not pass for pigs of knowledge."[34]

Activists and popular educators assumed swine personas like Brother Grunter, Porculus, Gregory Grunter, Pigabus, Old Bristle Back, Gruntum Snorum, and Spare Rib.[35] A periodical devoted to grappling with questions of politics and philosophy in a form accessible to less-educated classes proudly called itself *Pig's Meat, or Lessons for the Swinish Multitude*. Olivia Smith points out that "by vividly defining a large part of the population as brutish and inarticulate, Burke provoked them into speech."[36]

In the pejoratively intended expression "swinish multitude," many of its targets recognized how they were being seen from "above"—as treacherous, shifty, shiftless, dirty, greedy, uncultivated, inarticulate, and brutish:

> Being called "swine" in public, well-publicized discourse—comparable to the myriad references to the "mob" as vulgar, bestial, or monstrous, often found in elite literature—broke the old forms of subordination and deference, seemed to free the people by telling them what they probably already knew about how they were seen from "above." . . . The French Revolution shifts the moral axis, and awakens an audience to the demonizing quality of language and imagery. Still, rather than internalizing the sign, in self-disgust, many took it as a form of recognition. There was an activating quality to such rhetoric . . .[37]

This process took its course at precisely the point when poets and thinkers were calling for a new way of dealing with animals, sometimes out of humanistic respect for animals, sometimes as part of training in class-specific morality by means of children's literature.[38] True gentlemen did not torture animals. The lack of self-control exhibited by children would harm them in their later dealings with underlings. This metaphor spilled off the page into real life and became part of the actual development of solidarity with the situation of animals.

The vegetarianism of some of the advocates of the time had a slant that may seem surprising today. The political activist John Oswald, for example, had travelled in India and been a member of the Jacobin Club for four years; he died defending the revolution in 1793. His prominent friend Thomas Paine addressed him: "Oswald, you have lived so long without tasting flesh, that you now have a most voracious appetite for blood."[39] The only blood that this defender of the revolution wanted to consume was the blood of the enemies of democracy, not of penned-in or free-ranging pigs.

MULTITUDES BEYOND STATE AND PEOPLE

For Neocleous, the swinish multitude is undead, it can neither historically nor analytically be made to disappear. It comprises both the productive and the destructive aspects of living labour: "We might say that the proletariat is an entity which cannot be killed because the bourgeois order requires it to be living, but which as a mob cannot be assimilated into the current stable order—it is essentially disorderly."[40]

Pigs, never fully domesticated, became the unruly doppelgänger of the insurrectionists, because they occupy an ambivalent position in culture and society: "They belong not only to the house, but also to wilderness, to forest and swamp; they are considered symbols of fertility, but also of death and boundary-crossing. Their domestication remains precarious."[41]

The concept of the multitude has experienced a political vogue since the publication of Antonio Negri and Michael Hardt's *Empire* and its successor *Multitude*.[42] Translated literally, the Latin word *multitudo* means something like "quantity." In contrast to "mass" or "crowd," it does not mean a merging into a greater whole. *Multitudo* is distinct from a "people" to the extent that a "people" is understood as constituting of a nation. But it is also distinguished from "population" insofar as this is understood as the object of biopolitical governing activity within capitalist economies. The term "multitude" is set against "the state"; it denotes the production of acts of resistance and qualities of resistance through irreducible multiplicities. The multitude is a storm of passions, relations, and understandings that cannot be reduced to the number one—the state sovereignty of the Leviathan, as we encounter it in Thomas Hobbes's writings. If we read there, as a justification of state sovereignty "from above," that man is a wolf to man, then from a plebeian-porcine perspective "from below" it can be said with equal justification: man is a pig to man. The multitude is that from which no state authority can be derived: "but, like all modes of being, it is ambivalent, or, we might say, it contains within itself both loss and salvation, acquiescence and conflict, servility and freedom."[43]

What was shown by the swinish multitude as a concept and the lived praxis of animals and humans at Smithfield Market and in New York was the political power and the resistance of aggregates that included animals.[44] This appears to be a special case—yet resistance from those not considered to be sovereign citizens in full possession of their mental and physical powers is actually more the rule than the exception.

A REVOLT OF NERVES

This sort of resistance comprises the "exhausted self," which in the face of the exigencies of modernity and the workplace loses interest in interest itself: depression as the final emergency brake of the overwhelmed subject is no good as a slogan for political organizing, but it does point to forms of resistance that even the affected subject may be entirely or partly unaware of.[45] You feel empty and lacking any drive, nothing makes sense anymore, and a total lack of motivation sets in. Sometimes this has more to do with capitalism than with lack of exercise, poor nutrition, or carelessly filling out priority charts to help you get a grasp on life.

What in soldiers is called post-traumatic stress disorder (PTSD), an interaction of genetic and social influences, also occurs in pigs, where it is called porcine stress syndrome (PSS). One symptom of PSS is caudophagia, that is, tail biting. Pigs bite off those curly tails that advertisements like to display. To cope with this, many piglets have their tails "docked" as a precaution, which means removing the last third of their tails. Melanie Joy writes:

> Other symptoms include rigidity, panting, anxiety, blotchy skin and sometimes sudden death. Like humans who have endured solitary confinement and other tortures in captivity, pigs have engaged in self-mutilation and have been found repeating the same nonsensical behaviors over and over again, sometimes thousands of time a day; the animals are literally driven insane.[46]

If you can't defend yourself any other way, you go crazy. Then there's nothing they can do with you. This does not mean that people (or pigs) who are suffering from depression, and therefore behave in ways that render them unfit for gainful employment (or being eaten up), do this according to a plan. In both cases it is a revolt of body and mind against what is unbearable.[47]

GRAMSCI IN TIMES OF BIOSECURITY: PIG SOULS

In the age of avian flu, mad cow disease, and swine fever, the industrial animal body distends far beyond the tiny confines of its enclosure in an animal factory: wind and water carry microscopic particles of saliva, blood, feces, semen, and bacteria out into the world. Despite all hygiene regulations, these animal components settle in the ears and noses, under the fingernails and in the hair of agricultural workers, spreading to various agricultural facilities or various sections of the same facility, thus endangering the precious stock of factory animal species. This, at least, is the biocapitalist fear, which strives to protect itself from such contagions with "biosecurity" measures.

The anthropologist Alex Blanchette conducted field research in those areas of the Great Plains where most of the pigs born and killed in the US exist, investigating the social impacts on people who work there.[48] In the current regime of biosecurity, employees have to sign contracts specifying that no two coworkers of the pig factories are allowed to live in the same neighbourhood. In economically underdeveloped regions, this means either unemployment or separation from other employed family members that can last for years. The sociality of individual workers and their families thus becomes a source of danger for the precarious way of life of the industrialized pig. Sharing a beer or a tea in a park, or the number of showers taken at home, becomes the object of risk algorithms and labour law inspections.

With this, the phenomenon that Gramsci identified in connection with the development of Fordist industrialism, the (conformist) vetting of workers' leisure time by industrial spies to make sure that their family life is orderly, has reached its end in the post-Fordist economy of today. Not having a conventional family life is now a prerequisite for employment, even on the lowest levels of production.

YOU ARE PART OF THE SOLUTION, PART OF THE PROBLEM, OR PART OF THE LANDSCAPE

According to Blanchette, what is emerging here is a biocapitalistic agriculture that may well attribute an infinitesimal value to the individual pig, but which places the reproductive activities of the industrialized pig species, such as birth and growth, above bourgeois-humanistic values like the autonomy, freedom, and private sphere of human beings. Therefore Blanchette calls the forms of labour in these areas, such as the soy plantations of Paraguay or the fruit-growing regions of the American west coast, "posthuman labor." This also complicates the geochronological thesis of the Anthropocene, because the replaceable individual human being loses out to the irreplaceably valuable pig, soy, or fruit species.

Blanchette's research does not aim to develop a philosophical post-humanism that critiques capitalist forms of production "from the outside"; rather it tries to probe into the material forms of posthuman labour regimes within agro-capitalist practices. Although Blanchette's insightful work published in 2015 represents the state of the art in anthropological research in this field, it exhibits some epistemic weaknesses. In presenting his research at a conference in Detroit that I attended,[49] Blanchette included photographs of a phenomenon that is apparently not uncommon in pig production. The sows who are made to relentlessly give birth to piglets can only lie down or stand up in their cages, but can never turn around to make social contact with their offspring. They repeatedly try to run into the metal struts in front of them, sometimes until they succumb to their injuries, but this rarely happens, thanks to the ingenious technology of the cage.

Blanchette regards this phenomenon as a mental tic stemming from the repressive conditions the pigs are kept in. It never seems to occur to him that this could be a form of resistance, the last resort of the mother sow—a suicide attempt. The resistance of anthropology to the thought of swinish resistance would perhaps be too great.

Contrary to Alain Ehrenberg's much-discussed thesis that modernity has begotten a psychophysical surfeit of autonomy, the suspicion arises that it is exactly the opposite case with these reproductive sows: there is no longer even the freedom to turn for a moment towards the only purpose of their existence—their own piglets.

In his study of suicide in modernity, *Das Leben nehmen* (To Take One's Own Life), Thomas Macho asks: "Can animals really not commit suicide?"[50] His answer at least is unambiguous: "The last border-drawing between humans and animals—in the shape of the thesis that humans are the only animals who can commit suicide—is a recursive effect, as if the final result of a whole series of wars and demarcations against animals, and humans' own animality."[51]

THE BIRTH OF THE FACTORY

> Even when dead, the hog largely refuses
> to submit to the machine.
> —Sigfried Giedion

In the writings of the sociologist Max Horkheimer there is a conceptual image bearing the simple title "Skyscraper." In this short text, Horkheimer encapsulates his understanding of society in the architectural image of a cathedral of capital, the skyscraper. At the very top Horkheimer positions the various groups of managers and owners fighting each other. Under them, the political, military, and academic elites have installed themselves, followed by tradespeople, proletarians, and the ill. Below that we find colonial mass misery, which transcends all understanding, until the reader reaches the skyscraper's basement.

> Below the spaces where the coolies of the earth perish by the millions, the indescribable, unimaginable suffering of the animals, the animal hell in human society, would have to be depicted, the sweat, blood, despair of the animals. . . . The basement of that

> house is a slaughterhouse, its roof a cathedral, but from the windows of the upper floors, it affords a really beautiful view of the starry heavens.[1]

The skyscraper as a model was in no way an innocent metaphor, but itself a controversial topic of city-planning and architectural debates of that time—especially in Germany.[2] Coming out of the tradition of materialism with the Marxian idea of the economic base and social superstructure, the image means not only that many animals in the world of humans are suffering horribly, but that this sort of treatment of animals is an individual and social rehearsal of domination.

Horkheimer's longtime intellectual companion, Theodor Wiesengrund Adorno, noted in *Negative Dialectics*, his major philosophical work, published in 1966, that the man who was able to recall what struck him in the words "Luderbach" ("carcass brook") and "Schweinstiege" ("pig stile")

> might be closer to absolute knowledge than Hegel's chapter in which readers are promised such knowledge only to have it withheld with a superior mien. The integration of physical death into culture should be rescinded in theory—not, however, for the sake of an ontologically pure being named Death, but for the sake of that which the stench of cadavers expresses and we are fooled about by their transfiguration into "remains."
>
> A child, fond of an innkeeper named Adam, watched him club the rats pouring out of holes in the

courtyard; it was in his image that the child made its own image of the first man. That this has been forgotten, that we no longer know what we used to feel before the dogcatcher's van, is both the triumph of culture and its failure.[3]

Anyone who is familiar with the real semantic world bound up with the geographical names "Luderbach" and "Schweinstiege" understands more than could ever come from grappling with Hegel's absolute knowledge. This seems somewhat enigmatic even by Adorno's standards—what can he have meant?

Both place names come from Adorno's Frankfurt. The "Luderbach" is a southern tributary of the Main River near the Schweinstiege, an old term for a fenced-in area near what is today Frankfurt's Rhein-Main Airport. Long before Adorno was born, pigs were driven annually into the "Schweinstiege," a sort of corral or dugout. Until this herding together, however, the pigs lived free in the forest. Only for fattening were a certain number of them penned in and eventually slaughtered. The containment and confinement of the pigs in "dungeons of society-building"[4] by means of the increasing rationalization and economization of the livestock industry was already advanced by the time of Adorno's youth. Since for Adorno the development of modern rationality was connected with the subjugation of inner and outer nature, the spatial disappearance of pigs that were once frolicking in the woods seemed to him a more impressively visceral certainty than Hegel's spelling out of absolute knowledge.

In the image of adults' alienation from childlike sympathy for rats and dogs, we encounter the thought often articulated by Adorno and Horkheimer that the genesis of bourgeois subjectivity had to inure people to too much "feminine" emphasis and "childish" imitation: "Humankind has had to do terrible things, until the self, the identical, goal-oriented masculine character of the human was formed; and something of this is repeated in every childhood."[5] A person disciplined in this way, although a material and finite being, is up against "too much" nature; therefore the memory of his or her "natural" birth, which is shared with animals, remains a structural insult to the narcissistic ego. Likewise, the human cadaver resembles animal cadavers too much, which accounts for the many rituals intended to transform the dead human body into a corpse. The "stink of the cadavers" is abhorrent because it recalls this shared corporeality.

Elsewhere, Adorno ascribes the remark to Bertolt Brecht that culture is "a palace built out of dogshit."[6] The abhorrence of dog excrement also arises to a certain extent from the awareness that one's own excretions are not much different from those of any dog, and one's own *ultimate* corporeality is not much different from that of any dying animal. The outpourings of the mind and the artifacts of culture help us to forget this over and over again. The skyscraper is just such a palace of the amnesia of shared creatureliness. The view upward to the seemingly eternal stars consoles us in our knowledge that we too will decompose someday.

PORCOPOLIS

Horkheimer's choice of the concrete skyscraper image perhaps had something to do with a personal perspective, because from 1954 to 1959 he held a guest professorship in Chicago, the city that proudly called itself first Porcopolis and later Bovine City. The names come from Chicago's role, starting at the end of the nineteenth century, as the world's biggest slaughterhouse and meat processor. Chicago was the city with the first skyscrapers, financed with money from the slaughterhouses and meat markets. In this case, the now-proverbial suffering of the animals to be slaughtered, and their processed bodies, was in fact the economic basis for putting up those high-rises.

A hot-tempered cow is said to have been involved in these processes of world history. According to a local legend, the Great Fire of 1871, which reduced a third of Chicago to ashes, could be traced to an "until then unremarkable cow."[7] Mrs. O'Leary, the cow's legal owner, was trying to milk her on an unusually hot Sunday evening when, with one firm kick, the wilful beast knocked over the lantern illuminating the stall, thus unleashing a hellish inferno that consumed people, animals, and structures alike.[8]

The rebuilding of Chicago in the following years helped to modernize the city and attracted architects who saw it as a laboratory for urban innovation. For instance, they designed the Reliance Building as a harbinger of the "international style" that would leave its mark on the architectural aesthetics of the twentieth century. Skyrocketing real estate prices and new fire safety regulations led in 1884 to the construction of the world's first skyscraper, the Home Insurance Building, which also housed the offices of the legendary meat industrialist Philip Armour. It was his meat processing company whose world-famous motto was "We feed the world." This is more than just a marketing slogan: the Union Stockyards of Chicago did in fact process most of the meat in the United States well into the 1920s—more than any other place on earth. The Union Stockyards achieved this success only through a feverish drive to innovate that made them into a laboratory for modernity.

In any case, Adorno and Horkheimer's insights into and reflections on the human-animal relationship, which are scattered across many writings but found in concentrated form in *Dialectic of Enlightenment*, were long the most consistent and most radical products of Marxist thinking on these questions. Even today, many of these thoughts are highly stimulating. Except that in the pair's social-theoretical thinking, animals always appear even more wretched and objectified than humans in industrial societies already are. The latter appear inescapably caught in the extensive nexus of delusion of the culture industry in particular and class-organized society in general. It is even worse for animals because they don't have the solace of the culture of bourgeois society, no matter how questionable it may be. This extremely pointed victimology may have something to do with Adorno and Horkheimer's tendency towards cultural pessimism regarding change in modern societies, or with their always rather elitist understanding of politics, or with their institutional orientation, or else with the fact that, having been trained in philosophy, they schlepped too much liberal-humanist baggage on their intellectual travels. In any case, history for them appears as an inexorable result of philosophical ideas that always carry within them the germ of terror. With animals, then, everything is just more frightening and hopeless.

MECHANIZATION TAKES COMMAND

Another book written around the same time as Adorno and Horkheimer's *Dialectic of Enlightenment* might help shed some light on overlooked aspects of this mélange: Sigfried Giedion's *Mechanization Takes Command* (1948).[9] Giedion, who studied mechanical engineering in Vienna and art history in Munich, was virtually the modernist ideal type of an engineer well versed in art history. He was the longtime general secretary of the Congrès Internationaux d'Architecture Moderne (CIAM, International Congresses of Modern Architecture) and considered an ambassador of international high modernism. Generations of architecture students read his books. Stanislaus von Moos writes in the afterword of the German translation: "*Mechanization Takes Command* is not a book *about* modernity—it is a book *of* modernity."[10]

The project Giedion develops here was conceived as "a contribution to anonymous history"—the subtitle of the book. He is interested in inventions and countless improvements in technical processes which, while they have permeated our everyday culture, could not point to a famous creator. "The inventor as hero disappears in a vast multitude of tradespeople, tinkers, obscure businesspeople, and engineers," writes Hans Magnus Enzensberger.[11] Like Giedion's *Mechanization Takes*

Command, the *Dialectic of Enlightenment* was written in exile in the United States. Despite enormous differences between the two works, it makes sense to consider them in relation to each other—because in *Dialectic of Enlightenment*, one central theme is also the effects of industrial mechanization and standardization on the constitution of subjectivity in relation to aesthetic developments in the United States as an especially advanced form of capitalist socialization.

For Douglas Tallack, Giedion's cultural pessimism is less extreme than Adorno and Horkheimer's because of the difference in their cultural subject areas: "Architecture is a material Art form, and architecture and planning are more clearly in the public domain than literature or music, which members of the Frankfurt School tend to rely on as aesthetic bulwarks against mass culture, particularly American mass culture."[12]

Giedion traces the mechanization of simple and complex skilled trades—from metalworking, to agriculture and food production, to the design of furniture, household appliances, and bathrooms. Giedion does not wish to be comprehensive; rather, the attempts at mechanization are viewed in exemplary case studies grouped by topic, with an overwhelming abundance of empirical material and visual artifacts. As a passionate participant in contemporary movements, impartiality was not part of his journalistic interventions—Giedion was writing not as a neutral expert about a praxis different from his own investigations, but as a proponent of the modernist movement itself. This comes out in how "generously" important areas of mechanization are not discussed at all (e.g., military equipment, photography) or only barely touched on (art, architecture).

His technological histories of the sometimes audacious attempts to mechanize kneading, baking, or mowing also produced a "History of the Resistance of the Living," of the "organic," against attempts to mechanize its processing in emergent capitalism. For instance, Giedion describes the highly complex constitution of flour and dough, which long impeded the mechanization of bread production—and, using a wide range of sources, he documents the manifold attempts to mechanically master bread. But even if Giedion's genealogy of mechanization, with its many asides, cleverly inserted details, and hundreds of illustrations, is an extremely entertaining and rewarding read even seventy years after it was written, his tracing of almost all mechanizing trends of the present day back to the Middle Ages remains less than convincing.

The passages that have been emphasized by many commentators, and which even today are the most fascinating ones in the book, are devoted to the resistance of animals against being integrated into mechanization. These observations are concentrated in a chapter that plays a special role within *Mechanization Takes Command*, to be presented in more detail below: "Mechanization and Death: Meat."[3]

This chapter not only contrasts structurally with the other parts of the book, it is also its dialectical centrepiece. Giedion's thesis about the resistance to mechanization of the living reaches its most pointed conclusion in the resistance of living and dead animals to the mechanized slaughterhouse. It also reveals how grim industrial society is, because if the sun is reflected in a coffee spoon, as the book's motto has it, then the horrors of the twentieth century cast their long shadow forward from the slaughterhouses of Chicago, whose profits built the world's first modern skyscrapers.

WORLD LABORATORY OF CAPITALIST MODERNITY

Before Chicago, Cincinnati had the role of the centre of the trading and slaughter of animals in the United States.[14] Essential to this were Cincinnati's access to waterways and its geographical position in the north central United States, which together had first made possible the wide separation in space of production and consumption. The relationship of capital, transit times, and biological reproduction was more closely integrated than ever before. Successes in breeding produced animals that were ready for slaughter as early as their second year of life. Whereas fat summers and lean winters had previously determined the work and life rhythms of both humans and animals, the construction of grain elevators and the use of hay for fodder allowed the cyclical, concrete temporalities of biological reproduction to be increasingly adapted to the linear, abstract temporalities of capitalist regimes of accumulation.[15]

The animals themselves varied as well: cows with long legs could be driven over long distances—without significant weight loss, if cared for properly. Pigs were ideal animals for settlements since they ate everything imaginable, gained weight quickly, and produced abundant offspring. On the other hand, pigs were considered more stubborn or uncooperative than cattle and, given their short legs, they quickly lost weight over long distances. That's why there are no pigboys, only cowboys.

It was common practice to sew shut the eyes of especially obstinate pigs, since their sociality made them follow their fellow swine anyway. Cultural customs also had a role in shaping these processes; for example, beef was usually consumed fresh, while pork was cured and eaten much later as sausage, bacon, or ham.[16]

The main problem now was that without human intervention, dead animals went the way of all flesh and became inedible and unmarketable. The geographical, social, and physiological conditions made early winter the peak time for marketing and killing, since during this time the animals normally had their highest slaughter weight, and soon afterward the waterways would hardly be navigable. On the transport of living and dead animals, Giedion writes:

> The meat was either moved on the hoof or shipped, salted in barrels, down the Mississippi. Later on, when Chicago gained ascendancy in the 'sixties, the cattle were loaded into freight cars to be moved East; finally, at the beginning of the 'eighties, the supply system of today was set up, and refrigerator cars distributed the dressed carcasses to the various centers of consumption. From these beginnings developed the largest industry of the United States, as measured by turnover, $3.3 billion (in 1937), and with a production of some 50 million pounds a day.[17]

Chicago's rise as the global metropolis of meat at a scale that far outstripped Cincinnati began in the early 1860s, when railways could deliver the animals and the meat processing plants soon followed. In 1875, a new tin was introduced into which the meat could be pressed into a cake and preserved, "in a palatable condition . . . cooked, ready to be sliced and eaten."[18] Under the marketable name "corned beef," this pressed meat has survived to this day. Packed without bones and gristle into a handy small container, canned meat achieved a weight savings for transport of one to three compared to fresh meat—roughly the same ratio as refrigerated meat versus live animals.

In the third phase of Chicago's rise, in the early 1880s refrigerator cars led to the capture of the national and global markets. Now meat that had been killed hundreds of miles away cost less than local quality product could be sold for: the butcher turned from a tradesman into a salesman, and the meat processing sector became a global industry—the largest of its time.

At first, the Exchange Building in Chicago was where world grain prices were set, and then it became the largest shipping hub for animals and processed animal products. From here, connections to grain producers, livestock owners, and slaughterhouses spun a new kind of network that controlled the movement and processing of meat across the United States and ultimately altered the consumer behaviour of millions of people by means of refined workflows and new refrigeration technologies.

The result was an increasing interpenetration of city and countryside—cattle on long drives in Texas, ranches that had sprung up in Wyoming, cattle towns in Kansas and feedlots in Illinois

... all became linked in a new animal landscape that was governed as much by economics as by ecology. Considered abstractly, it was a landscape in which the logic of capital had remade first nature and bound together far-flung places to produce a profound new integration of biological space and market time. . . . Animals' lives had been redistributed across regional space, for they were born in one place, fattened in another, and killed in still a third.[19]

The combination of refrigeration technology and rail transportation emancipated the slaughterhouses from the areas around them. Animals no longer had to be shipped alive and then killed and butchered in scattered localities. Now one single integrated profitable industry could inspect, purchase, kill, and cut up animals in one place and send them to far-off butchers, who were now responsible only for final processing and retail sales.

Transporting only the most profitable animal parts instead of the whole body reduced transportation costs and minimized losses from the living animals themselves. Assets were not lost to overheating of the animals in transport, nor could profits be reduced by the transported animals refusing to feed. Injuries caused by other animals during shipment could also be avoided: "Flesh as money became the new and dominant equation."[20]

And so the most important hub for the traffic in animal bodies became the largest slaughterhouse in the world. Meat production, which before had usually been local and decentralized, became the most centralized and most international industry in the world.

The space of biological production and reproduction, with its temporal and geographical rough spots, became the smooth space of market-based production. Profitability, however, grew not from the increased efficiency of animal production itself, but from its collateral benefits: huge quantities accumulating centrally now not only made it *possible* to profitably market by-products that had been negligible in decentralized animal slaughter—it was even *necessary*. William Cronon, who analyzed the accounting records of the meat baron Armour, comes to a surprising conclusion: "Only by selling by-products could the packers turn this losing transaction into a profitable one."[21]

In Cincinnati most of the body parts of pigs—except for ham, shoulder, side, and belly—had been thrown after dismembering into the Ohio River. But in Chicago this logic was reversed: the animal leftovers regarded as garbage everywhere else were transformed in the slaughterhouses into glue, lard, candles, soap, and brushes, which could then come back as the all-important capital yield.[22]

Thus, in spite of all the effort, a single animal brought practically no profit. Even the best quality meat by itself would have been a money-loser. Only the exploitation of as many parts as possible, including what were once waste products, combined with the millionfold multiplication of their aggregated quantities, made the meat barons of Chicago into millionaires.

What people nowadays like to hold up as a contrast to the waste of the throwaway society—the use of every last part of the animal in small-scale Indigenous societies—turns out on closer inspection to be the logic of capitalist industry itself, which from its beginnings became lucrative via indirect profits from the large-scale exploitation of waste.

THE BIRTH OF THE ASSEMBLY LINE

The bottleneck of early winter, the point when animals were most profitable and could be transported on the rivers after slaughter, had led first in Cincinnati to great efforts to slaughter and butcher the animals more quickly and efficiently. From 1850 on, killing and dismemberment were already consolidated under one roof: "All other considerations were subordinated to the question: How to secure an uninterrupted production line?"[23]

No other area was the focus of so many attempts at optimization as "the one that sought to incorporate the living hog into the production line."[24] A hold-up at this point could bring the whole production process to a standstill. A fever gripped designers and tinkerers: the goal was now to finally mechanize the very killing and cutting up of animals. Giedion points to the high number of relevant patent applications from the mid-1860s to the early 1880s. But most of these attempts to improve the efficiency of killing and dismembering animal bodies with machines for catching, hanging, and flaying were colossal failures. They reminded Giedion of "medieval instruments of torture" that did not pass the field test in slaughter factories.

Again and again Giedion wonders why total mechanization, which had succeeded when it came to spinning, weaving, baking, and grinding grain, did not succeed in meat production. Not for want of enterprise and inventiveness, but because "a complex organic substance with its contingencies, its changing, easily vulnerable structure, is something other than a piece of amorphous iron."[25]

While in an earlier book[26] Giedion had celebrated the nineteenth century with respect to architecture, structural engineering, and construction, and had elevated the engineer into a new hero who also brought forth a profound aesthetic vocabulary, now when it came to the integration of the animal into production, everything was different—Giedion concedes outright: "To anticipate the answer: The engineer did not emerge victorious in this contest."[27] Who had forced the hero of the nineteenth century to his knees? According to Giedion, it was first the living animal, and then the dead one.

The intelligence of the engineers in simplifying the process of catching and hoisting by means of inclined planes foundered on the intelligence of the animals: "But the animals are quite likely to become suspicious before stepping on the inclined plane. Perhaps they will even resist being driven into the narrow passageway."[28]

Since practically all attempts at mechanizing the death and dismemberment of pig bodies had failed, efforts were concentrated on perfecting the human work process. In Cincinnati, for the first time, a movable rail was mounted on the ceiling, to pull the pigs through all stages of the slaughtering process with the aid of their own weight—around 1870, the prototype of the conveyor belt was born.

But because Cincinnati was "ashamed at first to trace its

wealth to pig packing," Giedion reports that only a single piece of pictorial evidence of the birth of the assembly line as an emblematic technology of the twentieth century has survived:

> ... a panorama painting, which the Cincinnati packers sent to the Vienna International Exhibition in 1873 and which ... records the hog-slaughtering process in all its stages, from the catching of the pig to the boiling of the lard. ... If one defines the assembly line as a work method wherein the object is mechanically conveyed from operation to operation, here is indeed its origin.[29]

While in Chicago in the 1850s approximately 20,000 pigs were killed and dismembered annually, Cincinnati processed about 330,000 pigs. Progress in railway construction, the interruption of trade by the outbreak of the Civil War, and the adoption of the "disassembly line" sealed Cincinnati's fate—in the 1870s Chicago, the new "Porcopolis," was killing and processing a million pigs a year.[30]

The invention of the assembly line in the slaughterhouses of Cincinnati is for Giedion the answer to the resistance of organic corporeality and animal subjectivity against industrial mechanization. On the comparable phenomenon of animals breaking out of the slaughterhouse, Markus Kurth writes: "Resistance is here understood less as intentional resistance to norms, but rather as something that bodies do—an unpredictability which results from gaps or contradictions in power, from mistakes of implementation."[31]

EVEN IN DEATH, THE PIGS RESISTED THE MACHINE

No machine was capable of killing and dismembering an animal that could not be standardized—human eyes and human hands were indispensable. Thus the focus shifted to perfecting the work process itself, in order to integrate animal bodies into their own mass-scale disintegration.

The human manual labour that machines could not replace, having been broken up into individual operations along a continuously running belt, became a high-performance machine. Because animal subjectivity and corporeality refused to be mechanized, the humans working here had to be organized into parts of a social machine. Giedion writes:

> Even when dead, the hog largely refuses to submit to the machine. Machine tools for planing iron, undeviating to the millionth of an inch, could be constructed around 1850. Down to the present day, no one has succeeded in inventing a mechanism capable of separating the ham from the carcass. We are dealing here with an organic material, ever changing, ever different, impossible to operate upon by revolving cutters. Hence all the essential operations in the mass production of dressed meat have to be performed by hand. For the speeding of output there was but one solution: to eliminate loss of time between each operation and the next, and to reduce

the energy expended by the worker on the manipulation of large carcasses. In continuous flow, hanging from an endlessly moving chain at twenty-four inch intervals, they now move in procession past a row of standing workers each of whom performs a single operation. Here is the birth of the modern assembly line.[32]

Whereas before Cincinnati and Chicago, three or four people could kill and dismember a pig within five hours, now more than 160 people were charged with specific tasks on the "disassembly line," and the journey of the pig through the vertical slaughterhouse now lasted only a fraction of the previously required time. Giedion notes that it was no coincidence that one of the few patents to pass its field tests was a device for manipulating the outside of the pig's body and removing its bristles: "Only in one operation was the machine introduced with at least partial success. Characteristically, this operation was not on the inside of the body. It was the task of mechanically removing hair and bristle." Through various processes the task of applying "firm pressure and adaptive elasticity" to the body was finally mastered.[33]

After the hogs, with their intelligence and sociality, had thwarted the engineers' plans, the delicate interior of their bodies remained a problem for mechanization, since the machinery crushed it, rendering it unmarketable. The pigs had resisted even beyond death.

FROM DISASSEMBLY LINE TO ASSEMBLY LINE

The birth of Fordism is usually dated to the year 1913, when in Dearborn, Michigan, Henry Ford set the first assembly line plant in motion. Ford had hit upon this idea after being deeply impressed by a visit to a Chicago slaughterhouse—above all by the speed of the moving chains and hooks that secured the animal "material" and continuously moved it to stationary workers who performed the same single steps over and over.

Applying production principles developed by Frederick Winslow Taylor, the scientific rationalizer of the work process, he developed a similar system for the Ford factory in Dearborn, but with one difference: Ford's automated production plants accelerated the assembly of a mechanical body instead of the disassembly of an animal body. The conveyor chain was transferred from the ceiling to the floor, but the splitting up of the operating procedures was retained.

The history of slaughterhouses reveals them to be a laboratory for industrial modernity. They are a part of those epoch-making processes that converted living time into working time. The specific social and physical technologies that they gave rise to can perhaps be best understood with the theoretical tools of a political and scientific movement that was also concerned with the resistance of life to being constrained by industry: workerism.

Workerist theory traced the technological developments of the capitalist economy back to the resistance of the living labour force. Autonomy means primarily the autonomy from capital (as well as from the parties, trade unions, and other groups within the working class) of the most advanced workers—in the sense of being employed in the most modern sections of industrial production.[34]

Workerism emerged as a critique of the objectifying representation of the role of living labour during the modernization process in postwar Italy: social democracy, labour unions, and communist movements neglected the migratory movements of southern Italian labourers who, having just been torn away from agriculture, were thrown into the most brutal working conditions of modern factories in northern Italy.

These workers did not raise moderate union demands, but instead there emerged, ignored by all, maladaptive forms of resistance like the destruction of the city centre of Turin in July 1962. The outermost horizon of intelligibility of previous communist militancy was too little for them: Who would want to "appropriate" or "take over" such a brutal factory? Sabotage or exodus were more obvious reactions. Workerism was born from theorizing about these struggles and the social and technological changes bound up with them. Workerists rejected gaping at economic developments in erotic rapture: not capitalism as such, as the sole powerful agent, was to be the basis of strategy and politics, but living labour power.

It was only the *reaction* of capital to the living labour force's varied forms of resistance (calling in sick, coming in late, taking breaks, and so on) and its desire-structures (not doing the same monotonous work every day, not being subject to rigid time rhythms for the rest of your life, not being the mute appendage of a machine, collaborative work instead of rigid hierarchies) that resulted in various forms of modernization:

the imperative of lifelong learning, the push for soft skills, and the omnipresence of project work.

In other words: capital, as dead labour and its technical, social, and economic dynamics, was no longer to be considered the only world-generating force that predetermined the battlefield coordinates. In opposition to this, living labour was to function as a methodological fulcrum, and the (frequently not union driven) resistance to the integration of human life into capitalist production was to be uplifted to the status of provocateur and originator of modernization.

CRAZY HORSES: MARX, MANAGER, MANÈGE

While there is something to be said for the workerist emphasis on resistant provocation of capitalist processes of modernization, it overshoots the target a bit to detect nothing but reactive appropriation on the capitalist side. But workerism is an important corrective to the objectifying prioritization of the agency of dead labour (capital). The strengths of workerism are especially evident with regard to animals, because nowhere does the zoo-political continuity of living labour prove stronger than in the resistance of animals.

In *Capital*, Karl Marx points out how animals with a mind of their own have caused problems for the production process: "Of all the great motors handed down from the manufacturing period, horse power is the worst, partly because a horse has a head of his own, partly because he is costly, and the extent to which he is applicable in factories is very restricted."[35]

The labour studies expert Kendra Coulter tells of resistant horses that retain a mind of their own even under "ideal" conditions of dressage riding:

> Horses are living beings. They have minds which on any given day can place them at different locations on a continuum of cooperativeness and disobedience, even after years of substantial and intensive training. They have moods which can change depending on weather, hormones, negative interactions with people or other horses, or any number of other factors. They have bodies which can feel pain, discomfort, stiffness, and so on.[36]

Recently, managers have been honing their social skills in "equine-assisted leadership training." The simple idea behind this booming training model: if you can get a horse to do what you want, you can do the same with your employees. What is presented here as a new, exciting experiential product on the professional development market is actually very old wine in new bottles. That is, the term "manager" as the leading figure for organization, administration, and supervision derives from the verb "to manage." In English, this first appears in the sixteenth century in the sense of *horse training* or *dressage*, inspired by the French *manège* (riding school).

A horse that totally resists dressage, a being that is completely unmanageable, would have to be called insane—it would be a "crazy horse."[37]

The possible objection that resistance in animals is a matter of instinct is either too weak or too strong. This would mean that instincts are biomechanical reflexes without any subjective dimension—a dog would then be more like a hairy robot that only superficially seems overjoyed when its owner comes home. Or else it would mean a complex process of biological impulses and social framing, because many animals are eager to play. Being able to take part in play, however, assumes the ability to distinguish between reality and fiction, to suppress impulses, instincts, and reflexes, at least temporarily—otherwise no game in the world would be possible.

Furthermore, all games not only require keeping to the rules, but they always have the potential to improvise as well, varying the playful gestures involved, that is, to creating something new.

TRAINED GORILLAS

The new forms of production were the subject of Antonio Gramsci's famous essay from the prison notebooks in which he introduced the concept of Fordism. The text with the title "Americanism and Fordism" (Notebook 4, 52) was originally titled "Animalism and Industrialism." Here Gramsci formulates the idea that the history of industrialism was a continual struggle against the element of "animality" in humans. In this context he quotes Frederick Winslow Taylor, who spoke of the worker as a "trained gorilla." Nicole Shukin finds Gramsci's first self-correction of the heading of his text, writing animals and animality out of the history of Fordism, emblematic for critical theorizing on the history of capitalism:

> Tracking how animal life is put into contradictory circulation as both a carnal and a symbolic currency implicates Fordism in a double logic of rendering overlooked by a long line of critiques that take the human, in the privileged figure of the labourer, as the focal historical subject of industrial capitalism.[38]

The analysis of the material and semiotic reality of these relationships could begin with Giedion's social history of technology, to which the analyses of the Frankfurt School seem deeply foreign in a liberating way. The Australian economist duo JK Gibson-Graham point out in their book *The End of Capitalism (As We Knew It)* that in critical theory building, capitalism has taken on the appearance of an almost omnipotent metasubject—which often obscures the view of the concrete analysis of economic and social contexts more than it serves it.[39]

Therefore, what is known is still a long way from being understood. Instead of reflexively asserting that the resistance of animals is not "whole" or "true," because that which must not be cannot be, we should reaffirm Marx's materialist insight that one must confront conditions with one's eyes open:

> Hence, nothing prevents us from making criticism of politics, participation in politics, and therefore real struggles, the starting point of our criticism, and

from identifying our criticism with them. In that case we do not confront the world in a doctrinaire way with a new principle: Here is the truth, kneel down before it! We develop new principles for the world out of the world's own principles.[40]

PROVINCIALIZING THE HUMAN

But why do Marxists often have difficulty seeing animals as more than mere implements? The post-colonial Subaltern Studies Group has worked out how within Indian Marxist historiography certain forms of resistance by women or the unlanded were made to disappear. Here, subalterns are those whose voice cannot be heard even in Marxist systems of thought because there is still no room in the architecture of this thinking, or else such room is structurally excluded. Within the political rationality of these schools, the resistance of certain persons was not intelligible.[41] This is epistemic violence, that is, the structural violence that inheres in systems of thought. With his book *Provincializing Europe* (2000), Dipesh Chakrabarty has presented a sustained critique of Eurocentric historiography of Marxist provenance.[42] Chakrabarty's point here is not to deny geopolitical relationships of dependency, but rather to place, not unintentionally, a sombrely coloured laurel wreath on the head of colonialism and its legacy. This means not merely "upending" the idealization of colonial predation by simply adopting the triumphant history unchanged and placing a minus sign before it.

In a way epistemically comparable to the colonized, animals are not just victims, but perpetrators as well. Animals are not only objects of human maltreatment under the sign of capitalism, but also biosocial entities whose history and struggles are bound up with those of humans in many ways. In critical solidarity with the project of decolonizing thought, what is at stake is nothing less than its continuation: the provincialization of humanity as the privileged figure and only subject of history and politics.

ANIMALS OF MIGRATION

The legacy of colonialism is also apparent today in worldwide migration movements: politically akin to the movement for the autonomy of migration, it is necessary to articulate the history of animals in capitalism as a history of struggles. Because migration was also long considered to be purely a game of "push" and "pull" factors. This means that there are factors that "push" humans out of the spaces of their daily lives, such as natural disasters and civil wars, or neocolonialism and the misery it promotes. To this are added factors that "pull" people in a particular direction: capital in need of labour power, national labour recruitment agreements, and so on. Between these two poles, migration as a force ceases to exist, it is moved but does not move itself, it has no life of its own, no world-generating power. Migrants appear here as mere victims of external powers. In misery at home, and then when they arrive in the West, all that is left to them is McDonald's, caregiving labour, and hyper-exploitation as wage depressors—ignored by labour unions and demonized by political parties. A continuity of victim status.[43] Not to forget the people smugglers who profit from all of this to boot.

The theoretical and political movement for the autonomy of migration, however, attempts to consider it from the perspective of the subjectivity of those affected and their struggles.[44] Migration is a profoundly social process; who can pay a human smuggler out of their own pocket? Entire extended families or half a village pool their resources to do so.

In transit, these migrant subjects stay in communication with each other and with their former homes, keeping informed, exchanging information, straining the borders of empires, storming the fortresses of "old" and "new" continents.

This means neither that this process is especially humane, nor that there aren't many victims. Migrants too are certainly not the new heroes. Heroes seem to be a thing of the past anyway. But when Russian migrants in Berlin quietly occupy vacant buildings en masse so they can live there temporarily, then this is eminently political—even if they don't hang flags out of the windows.

But let's stay with the people smugglers for a moment. They themselves are animals, or at least they appear to be:

> The coyote is more than a *canis latrans* in the borderline of USA and Mexico. It also designates all the commercial "guides" who are able to cross the

national borders and organize illegal migrational movements and undocumented mobility. British sailors call the elusive helpers of stowaway passengers "sharks"; in the Greek-Albanian borders their name is "korakia" (ravens). In Chinese they are called "shetou" (snakehead); a person who is as cunning as a snake and knows how to use his/her agile head to find a way through difficult situations.[45]

For Dimitris Papadopoulos, Vassilis Tsianos, and Niamh Stephenson, this "becoming animal" also takes place on the other side. When people destroy their identity papers to make it harder to identify and deport them:

> A body without a name is a non-human human being, an animal which runs. It is non-human because it deliberately abandons the humanist regime of rights. The UNHCR convention for asylum seekers protects the rights of refugees on arrival, but not when they are on the road. And we already know, the arrival has a longue durée, migration does not really concern the moment of arrival but the whole trip, almost your whole life. This is how migration solves the enigma of arrival. As the burners say in Leila Kilani's film (*Tanger, le rêve des brûleurs* Morocco/France 2002), if you want to cross the Spanish borders, it is not sufficient to burn your papers, you have to become a dog, to become an animal yourself.[46]

Animals appear not only to have an opportunistic relationship to the state. More than that: they can get in everywhere. When the Biosphere 2 was built in Arizona, the intent was to construct as self-sustaining a system as possible, as a model world for simulating the conditions on another planet. Everything was controlled, everything was monitored. Nevertheless, so-called crazy ants managed to get in, formed "super colonies," and spread throughout the hermetically sealed Biosphere 2. To this day, no one knows how they did it.[47]

Hence, placing one's hopes on a two-hundred-million-dollar scientific experiment does not seem advisable. Completely trusting people smugglers wouldn't be judicious either. But underestimating their power or importance would be just as big a mistake.

The point is to understand animals not as the ultimate losers of culture and capitalism, but as resistant agents within a non-innocent conflict. The whole assemblage of technologies for tagging and manipulating, of architectures of control and confinement, of hormones and calcium supplements, of aviaries and pens, of nets and baits would not be merely monuments to their misery, but proof of their monstrous power.

UNDERGROUND ECOLOGIES

The oncomouse eats Heidegger.
—Paul B. Preciado

In the big cities of the world, enormous amounts of natural and artificial hormones flow into the sewer systems and from there to sewage treatment plants, where they collect in tiny organisms like worms. These scurrying and scrabbling hormone snacks get fished out of the treatment plants and eaten by birds. Researchers from Cardiff University and the Max Planck Institute in Seewiesen, Germany, have studied the effect of these tidbits on the birds and discovered some astounding things: the birds didn't grow any extra limbs or sex organs (like we would expect in a *Simpsons* episode)—instead, the starlings being studied exhibited new forms of song. They not only sang longer, faster, and with more endurance, but they also had an expanded repertoire of songs. The birds doped up on human hormones were able to attract more sex partners than ever before.[1]

This seems counterintuitive. After all, we've learned from countless tragic David Attenborough documentaries that the existence of human beings has only brought misery upon the world of wild animals.

Becoming an icon is probably always a dubious sort of fame, but it is definitely so when it is an icon of extinction. Together with the woolly mammoth, the dodo, the aurochs, and the tyrannosaurus, the passenger pigeon is considered one of these "great icons of extinction."[2] If in the seventeenth and eighteenth centuries single flocks still comprised several billion passenger pigeons, the nineteenth century was gripped by a sort of hunting mania for these birds; their nesting sites were publicized by telegraph, and the birds were slain by the bucketload and shipped off by the carload:

> Passenger pigeons used to inhabit all the territories of the US and Canada. They appeared in the sky in such thick flocks that they literally blocked the sun. It grew dark like during an eclipse. The flying birds covered the whole firmament from one horizon to the other. Pigeon dung fell from the sky like snowflakes; the endless hum of wings recalled the whistling of storm winds. Hours went by, but the pigeons were still flying and flying, with neither the end nor the beginning of their marching column in sight. Nothing could divert this "squadron," innumerable as locusts, from its course—not shouts, not gunshots, not cannon fire. . . . Was it really possible to exterminate such a fantastic multitude of birds quickly? The sad fate of the passenger pigeon tells us that it is possible, if you take up this task in a clever way.[3]

Even belated attempts by conservationists that newly appeared on the scene could no longer help replenish the population by breeding individual pairs. These birds apparently needed those huge flocks of kin. A monument to the extinct bird bears the words of Aldo Leopold, a father of the conservation movement in the United States: "the bird could survive no diminution of his own furious intensity."[4]

The great number of scientists and authors who turned their attention to the passenger pigeon after its disappearance have bestowed upon the lively afterlife of the defunct bird the almost mythical character of an anti-phoenix. "The Passenger Pigeon is a wholly ironic version of the Phoenix: its death is reborn every time we discuss the bird. No matter how many times the bird's death is rehearsed, however, it can never be resuscitated. In a manner of speaking, the bird dies from death to death rather than dying from death into life."[5]

The last documented specimen became an individual on the eve of her death, which was also the death of her species: Martha, the last of her kind, died on September 1, 1914. In the months before her death in the Cincinnati Zoo, Martha was painted, photographed, and—that's how important she had become—filmed.[6]

What is rare is eroticized as precious, which is even more true of what will soon not exist at all. Being able to experience the last of a species gives us the narcissistic feeling that we are enjoying some special privilege, being a witness to an exclusive event—like the last-ever performance of some geriatric rock band on its actual farewell tour. If you arrive only to find out, against all expectations, that a slew of additional performances and whole tours are planned, the result may not be relief, but frustration.

BERGHAIN ECOLOGIES

Ruined civilizations and zoological fossils are the past tense form of this nostalgic spectacle. The Renaissance was a feast of this sort of ruin mania, and since then the rapt contemplation of historical ruins has been part of Europe's cultural heritage. Maybe one motive for this coveting of ruins lies in the suspicion that modern promises of happiness leave much to be desired. Whereas you could once hope for fulfillment on the other side, this-side-ification has been accompanied by a nostalgic swing to things of the past. What enthralled the Renaissance about the Roman and Greek relics now enthralls our contemporaries in the Rust Belt along the US-Canada border, where the most-photographed modern-day ruins are to be found—the post-industrial halls of former automobile production plants in the American city of Detroit. The going term for touristic delight at visiting these landscapes of urban decay, and for the widespread circulation of photographs of these sites, is *ruin porn*.

But Detroit is also one of the birthplaces of techno, which in its fabric-softened form as electronic dance music has reached the pinnacle of mainstream entertainment. The Berlin techno club Berghain, on the other hand, flies the flag of the underground.[7] But the underground of the underground can't be found in Berghain's club room, nor upstairs in the Panorama Bar, nor downstairs in the Lab.Oratory. The "real" underground is found farther down, in the sewers. Because sooner or later all the drugs that get consumed up above have to get out, too—they flow down through the sewer system, where the animals that live there take a bath in veritable showers of hormones and other potent molecules. There is no research on this particular habitat of urban ecology, but why shouldn't there be rats here, hopped up on amphetamines and raving to themselves, or cockroaches copulating at high frequencies, or snuggledrunk toads on MDMA sliding against each other, or psychoactively dissociated mice, with ketamine coursing through their bloodstreams?

At one time, the club was the space of another life. Certain details still recall this: if you've had enough of racism, you only have to visit a club to experience how members of the majority, high on ecstasy, convincingly reassure the immigrant woman bathroom attendant how awesome she is. But regardless of the organizers' intentions and particular evenings or events, the coordinate system that clubs exist in has changed. In the past, the weekend might have functioned as distinct from the logic of gainful employment, but today free evenings are used to practise everything that's expected at the new workplace: capacity for enthusiasm and identification with the work process, social skills and the ability to work in a team, and conveying ease while doing hard work. In short: Saturday is the new Monday.

PORN, PHARMA, POWER

Paul B. Preciado has coined the term *pharmacopornographic regime* for the new regimen of subjectivity.[8] The development of the contraceptive pill and the publication of the first issue of *Playboy* magazine are symbolic milestones for this new form of power. The pharmacological aspect of this form of power includes the mass administration of and self-medication with biomolecular entities. Estrogens for skin management or Ritalin for treating children with attention deficit disorder are just as much a part of this as the change in mass sexuality through the discovery of the erectile effects of Viagra, or the large-scale ingestion of antidepressants, mood enhancers, and sedatives. The circulation, consumption, and DIY production of sexy images constitute the pornographic pole of this regime (from the first glossy magazine with Marilyn Monroe's likeness to today's Instagram images).

Animals, especially animal body parts and bodily fluids, were raw materials in the development of the biomolecular pole of this form of power, which no longer only disciplines us from the outside in the form of architectures and orthopaedics acting upon the body, but also infiltrates our bodies as aspects of techno-bio power and controls us as we regulate ourselves with potent molecules:

> The success of contemporary techno-science consists in transforming our depression into Prozac©, our masculinity into testosterone, our erection into Viagra©, our fertility/sterility into the pill, our AIDS into Tri-therapy without knowing which comes first; if depression or Prozac©, if Viagra© or an erection, if testosterone or masculinity, if the pill or maternity, if Tri-therapy or AIDS.[9]

Sigmund Freud's first scientific paper already dealt with the question of sex hormones in fish, and Jacques Lacan's famous treatise on the mirror stage couldn't do without considering the development of sex hormones in pigeons. But historically it was the scientific disciplines of endocrinology, sexology, and psychology that were the midwives to this regime in the second half of the twentieth century. The scientific work connected with these disciplines was only possible by means of vast numbers of animal bodies, whose sex glands were used for extracting hormones. This is why most hormone institutes were located near slaughterhouses. Only the discovery that estrogen is abundant in urine totally changed the earlier economy of extracting this precious substance.

PLEASURE POTENTIAL, BEYOND ANIMAL WELFARE

Alongside the countless studies pointing out the negative impacts of bioactive substances on the bodies and behaviour of animals, the time has come to pay attention to the pleasure potential of these biochemical resources for animals. Preciado terms this perverse-sounding potential for excitement *potentia gaudi*. This "orgasmic force" is an "endless capacity" that does for the pharmaco-pornographic ecology what "the force of work [did] in the domain of classical economics."[10] Animals were not only central to the testing and development of many medical drugs we take, but they were also often the raw materials for producing these substances. Animals' bodies were crucial for the emergence of the new power of hormones, so why should we, in the name of a dusty old concept of nature, refuse from the outset to let them participate in this power to improve singing skills or enhance pleasure?

Hormone-doped birds and bugs on drugs: that seems totally wrong. But maybe only because we've gotten used to certain notions of nature and naturalness. Fortunately, such notions can change with time, but this doesn't happen uniformly. When Conchita Wurst, the bearded but feminine artistic persona of the Austrian drag artist Thomas Neuwirth, won the Eurovision Song Contest in 2014, many progressive spirits rejoiced at Europe's open-mindedness. A few years earlier, just as many people got worked up about Michael Jackson (allegedly or actually) turning white. For some reason race has to bear the burden of "authenticity." Changing your religion, nationality, or gender seems to many to be a form of freedom. But for many people, the mere idea that a wealthy Black person would want to change the colour of his skin carried with it the aura of insufficient self-esteem or even betrayal.

Maybe we also don't want animals to step too far out of line and do things we deem inappropriate (= unnatural). But just as there is no true essence of art, nor a fundamental core of human nature, nor of womanhood or manhood, there is also no intrinsic canineness, and there is no intrinsic chickenness that is the same across time and space.

A cat living in a high-rise in Tokyo has different impressions and a different environment than a dog that accompanies an itinerant freetekno sound system from party to party. That's why talk of species-appropriateness makes so little sense: not only do individuals of the same species often exhibit very different preferences or behaviour—but completely dissimilar environments lead to dissimilar personalities and ways of reacting. Animals of the same species are not the same everywhere. And even animals are allowed to expand their consciousness, to experience different modes of perception, to become someone other than who they are.

A radio journalist once reported that when he opened the door to an urban squat, he was met with an extraordinary sight. There were DJs lying all around, recovering from the exhausting night. A small dog was standing on the chest of one of the sleepers, carefully licking drug residue from the DJ's nostrils. Then it jumped onto the next slumberer and feasted once again on the unused potential for stimulation. Sustainable resource management, you might call it. And why shouldn't canine nasal pilferage for the sake of getting high be "species appropriate"?

When recently, on an Internet forum for anti-fat-shaming activists, someone posted a photo of their corpulent dog, a small shitstorm erupted over the dog owner. The unanimous sentiment was that letting a dog get fat was extremely irresponsible. But why did those body activists so quickly turn into health fetishists as soon as they were talking about a dog? For humans, after all, they advocated vehemently for their right to their own bodies. What's more, the dog in the photo looked relatively happy, which the equally cheerful dog owner also emphasized. Maybe resentment towards nonconformist animals has to do with the way the ideology of pets as family members makes them into eternal children. (Hello, Norma Bates!) Grown-up animals are not human children.[11]

But intoxicated animal individuals aren't the only ones

who might profit from the increase in bioactive substances. Empirical studies suggest that Viagra might be an ally in the fight against the extinction of biological species. The sales figures for seal genitalia from Canada and caribou antlers from Alaska collapsed after the pharmaceutical concern Pfizer introduced Viagra in May 1998.[12] Both items are part of alternative and traditional medicine, and are also used to treat erectile dysfunction.[13] The same is true, for instance, of sea cucumbers, seahorses, geckos, and the green sea turtle, whose entire bodies, body parts (male genitalia), and body products (eggs) may be have been saved by the advent of Viagra.

One reason for this is that the effects of Western erection-enhancing drugs are quickly verifiable, as opposed to other mainstream medicines whose effectiveness is not immediately clear to the consumer. The other reason is price: Viagra, especially as a generic, is often cheaper than counterparts made from animal bodies.[14] Although sales figures are hard to determine for animal species that are banned because they're threatened by extinction, and the professional debate is not yet settled,[15] these results at least open up the seemingly ironic prospect that "chemicals" not only contribute to ecological problems, but could also be part of the solution.

IRONIC SPECIES PROTECTION

Self-irony is a popular virtue among enlightened people. But even decommissioned American poison gas factories can show an appreciation for irony. For more than forty years, the Rocky

Mountain Arsenal (RMA) in Colorado, owned by the US Army, had been producing nerve gas, mustard gas, napalm, white phosphorus, and similar substances that the Free World just seemed to need on a regular basis. In 1991 the arsenal surprisingly published a calendar with landscape photos documenting the rugged beauty of the area at the foot of the Rocky Mountains. The calendar, which was distributed to neighbours of the restricted military zone and to residents of the nearby city of Denver, bore the title "The Most Ironic Nature Park in the Nation . . ." The introductory text explained this unusual title:

> Flourishing wildlife, toxic waste, and an epic history make Denver's Rocky Mountain Arsenal the most ironic nature park in the nation. Legislation now pending before Congress could make it official. RMA's 17,000 acres—containing the former Army chemical weapons facility and Shell pesticide plant—are proposed as the nation's first wildlife refuge on a Superfund site [highly toxic areas to which government funds are allocated]. The prospect of millions of visitors at RMA calls for new thinking about "environmental education." RMA could help us learn about our history, the survival of nature in an urban-industrial environment, the realities of hazardous waste, and our hopes for the future.[16]

Goodbye dreadlocks and corduroy bellbottoms, farewell to practical clothes and that bicycle fetish: the new environmental activists are sporting crewcuts and manufacturing chemical weapons. Between times they want to discuss "our hopes for the future." As much as some of us would like to believe that the US Army has turned into a wildlife protection agency, this requires a closer look.

This area of approximately twenty-seven square miles was requisitioned by the US Army during World War II—the farmers living there had thirty days to leave the territory—and declared a restricted military zone. Here the Rocky Mountain Arsenal was built to develop, manufacture, and store chemical weapons, and later to dispose of them as well. Parts of the area were leased to Shell Oil and other manufacturers of highly poisonous pesticides for use in agriculture and home gardens. In 1984, the poison gas factory was closed, but over the years there have been many local complaints about the toxic contamination of the groundwater. In that same year, the US Army began a series of scientific studies of the soil and groundwater that discovered alarmingly high concentrations of toxic substances. This result was hardly surprising. In 1986, however, the military scientists were amazed to note that a dozen bald eagles had settled on the grounds. At that time, these birds were in acute danger of going extinct. Further investigation showed that the eagles were in the best of health.

A while later it was discovered that various animals, like pelicans and coyotes, had sought and found refuge in this contaminated zone: more than 330 animal species were counted in this small area, which the Army Corps of Engineers said encompassed "the most contaminated square mile on Earth."[17] The most toxic place in the US was also the place with the greatest diversity of species. Nature itself seemed to have become an ironist.

BIRDS & BOMBS

After the area had been declared a priority hazardous waste site, making substantial federal funding available, the first sections of the land were cleared of the worst toxins. In 1992, the Arsenal was closed and the law that the scenic calendar had hoped for became a reality. This law provided for converting certain sections of the territory into a nature park after further decontamination. In 2011 the time had come to open the visitor centre of the Rocky Mountain Arsenal National Wildlife Refuge, after two billion dollars had been spent on the most basic removal of toxins from the soil.

Jim Omans, the Marine Corps natural resource manager based in Washington, DC, explains: "The military is perhaps a natural ally with [conservation groups] because we seek the same things they seek." Their motives may be completely opposite—"We want it for training. They want it for critters"—but the important thing is that "we both want large unbroken areas filled with natural habitat."[18]

This bizarre success story of the weapons-to-conservation project had of course been more complicated—in the 1980s, Shell Oil, the army, and the Environmental Protection Agency had been at loggerheads over the extent of the necessary environmental cleanup. "In separate litigation, the state of Colorado was suing the Army and Shell, the Army was suing Shell, and Shell was suing its insurers. And federal agencies, developers, neighboring communities, and local environmentalists were at odds over what to do with the arsenal once the Army left. Bald eagles changed all that."[19]

The eagles' status as an endangered species that is also the official national animal and national bird (the United States has both, and it is the same animal), and which is emblazoned on the Great Seal of the United States of America, and is the national emblem (on all one-dollar bills), and which furthermore called up associations with a militaristic history, made it easier to come up with the plan for a nature refuge on poisoned soil. Amid legal and financial clashes over the extent of the environmental cleanup, this was the most affordable way out. That is, if a natural refuge was the intended use after the cleanup, the law required a much less thorough decontamination than it did for commercial use or human habitation. In this case, after all, people would only occasionally come into contact with the poisonous soil or drinking water. Besides, using it as a nature refuge meant that permission would be given to set up a hazardous waste storage site with 46 million cubic feet of contaminated soil on site, and the ground would only have to be decontaminated to a depth of three to six feet.

"SARINGETTI"

The secrecy that shrouds military areas also means that there is no clarity about what exactly is stored there. The generosity of the US Army in providing truthful information increased the discomfort of many local residents. They took the conversion into a wildlife refuge as an affront to their years of efforts to get a deeper (more than just six feet) decontamination of the area. The nature refuge remains controversial. Only in 1996, by directly contacting the Pentagon, could activists manage to get the word "Arsenal" included as part of the name on all signs, after the military authorities had tacitly removed it while the cleanup work was still going on. When in 2000 a bomb containing the extraordinarily powerful poison sarin (which was deployed by Chilean strongman Augusto Pinochet against his political opponents and presumably used in Iraq in 1988 against five thousand Kurds) was found in the decontaminated area, and the US Army tried to cover it up, the local press dubbed the natural park "Saringetti," an ironic reference to the Serengeti National Park in Tanzania.

Meanwhile, the visitor centre at the Rocky Mountain Arsenal National Wildlife Refuge, funded by Shell, has been engaged in historical greenwashing. The informational material on display at the site explains how at first nomadic Arapaho and Cheyenne lived here, and later farmers worked the land. After that, the area was used for war efforts and passed on to Shell, to boost the national economy. And now, nature was simply taking over again. The arsenal, which was built in all haste to try to catch up with the German chemical weapons program, the napalm bombs manufactured here that were dropped on Japan on March 9 and 10, 1945, and the arms race during the Cold War in general, to which the arsenal supplied armaments[20]—all of this appears in the harmless informational material of a marvellously ironic natural park as uniformly normal uses of the land, like the berry picking of nomadic peoples a few centuries earlier.

The rhetoric of the obliteration and eradication of human as well as non-human enemies predates the twentieth century, but only in that century was the technical and organizational capacity attained to fight the enemy extensively and faster than ever. As the US historian Edmund Russell has written:

> Annihilation of national and natural enemies had become realistic on a large scale, a reality both comforting and disturbing to people who lived in the post–World War II era. The twin insecurities raised by military and civilian technology illustrated that war and environmental change were not separate endeavors, but rather related aspects of life in the twentieth century. One of the best places to see these linkages made concrete was at Rocky Mountain Arsenal. There, using the same equipment, Shell made insecticides and the Chemical Corps made chemical weapons.[21]

The Rocky Mountain Arsenal National Wildlife Refuge raises an array of seemingly paradoxical questions. A complete decontamination and cleanup of the area would doubtless have spelled the end of the wildlife refuge. The idea of an animal preserve was pushed through by Shell, the military, and the political apparatus in order to save immense additional costs. Without this factor, the pressure to exploit this area economically would have been unstoppable. The environmental cleanup would have meant the end of the animals that had made the toxic dump their home.

RADIOACTIVE SPIRITUALITY

The Rocky Mountain Arsenal is a node within a larger network of similarly paradoxical places, like the Demilitarized Zone (DMZ) between North and South Korea. Conservationists there have been watching the progress toward peace between the two countries with mixed feelings, because the Demilitarized Zone has become a unique nature reserve for many endangered species.[22] For them, peace means death.

The park near Denver also brings up the question of how to deal collectively with highly toxic materials, because simply burying them is not the best solution. This is particularly true of radioactive waste, like that which contaminated another part of Colorado not far from the Arsenal. While the Arsenal lies ten miles northeast of Denver, fifteen miles northwest of the city are the Rocky Flats, where from 1952 to 1989, all detonators for US nuclear weapons were produced. After this area, which is used as a refuge by about 250 endangered animal species, had been environmentally remediated (under similarly controversial circumstances as the Arsenal), in 2007 it was declared the Rocky Flats National Wildlife Refuge and transferred from the military to the United States Fish and Wildlife Service. Rocky Flats is not accessible to the public, but the public tellingly calls it the "Rocky Horror Show."[23]

Julia Kristeva used the term "abject" to designate that

which is cast off or discarded. Slime or spiders are abjects that induce disgust. Other abjects are aspects of the world that we totally banish from our conscious thinking because they disturb us too much.[24] The literary theorist Timothy Morton invokes Julia Kristeva's abject in order to understand the Rocky Flats phenomenon.

> Ecological politics is bound up with what to do with pollution, miasma, slime: things that glisten, schlup, and decay. Should radioactive waste from the nuclear bomb factory at Rocky Flats be swept under the Nevada carpet of an objectified world, a salt deposit that was declared in the 1950s to be safe, but in the 1990s had been found to leak (the Waste Isolation Pilot Project, or WIPP)? . . . What does one do with the leakiness of the world?[25]

Morton sees the Nuclear Guardianship initiative founded by Joanna Macy as remarkable because it politicizes spirituality, "as not an escape from, but a taking care of, the abject." Nuclear Guardianship "assert[s] that substances like the plutonium whose release of poisoned light takes tens of thousands of years to cease, should be stored above ground in monitored retrievable storage; moreover, that a culture, indeed a spirituality, would have to grow up around the tending of this abject substance."[26]

Bafflement at the adjacent presence of what seems irreconcilable—the supremely artificial (radioactivity, hazardous waste) with the extremely natural (wild animals, biodiversity instead of industrial monoculture)—also occupies the environmental historian William Cronon:

> There is nothing natural, surely, about the arsenal's toxicity—and yet that toxicity is itself one of the most important things supporting the wild nature for which the place is now celebrated. The familiar categories of environmentalist thinking don't seem to work here, since we have no clear indication of what would be "natural" or "unnatural" to do in such a case.... The ability to blur the boundaries between "natural" and "unnatural" is precisely what makes the Rocky Mountain Arsenal and other found objects so useful for encouraging us to question our assumptions about what nature means and how we should relate to it.[27]

THE DISCRETE CHARM OF BOURGEOIS NATURE

At first blush, Morton's reflections on Nuclear Guardianship may recall that disturbingly beautiful scene in *Beneath the Planet of the Apes* (1970) where the survivors of a nuclear holocaust worship an atom bomb as a weapon of peace. But they also may remind us that "myth making" could qualify as a conscious government strategy to communicate with future generations. At least that's what the Human Interference Task Force, created by the Department of Energy in the 1980s and assigned to investigate the problems connected with base closures and the final marking of filled nuclear waste repositories, recommended for the "Waste Isolation Pilot Plant" in New Mexico.[28]

The likelihood of human interference was supposed to be minimized for ten thousand years, but material signs or even language might have deteriorated by then, so much so that it was not certain that any form of warning would be understood. Therefore the report suggested inventing folkloristic devices, in particular the combination of an artificially created and nurtured ritual-and-legend.[29] A "false trail" of accumulated superstition would steer the uninitiated away from the hazardous site, while the actual scientific truth of radiation and its implications would be entrusted to an "atomic priesthood," that is, a commission of knowledgeable physicists, experts in radiation sickness, anthropologists, linguists, psychologists, semioticians, and whatever additional expertise might be called for, now and in the future. Membership in this "priesthood" would be self-selective over time.[30]

The report concluded that the "best mechanism for embarking upon a novel tradition" was at present unclear: "Folklore specialists consulted have advised that they know of no precedent, nor could they think of a parallel situation, except the well-known, but ineffectual, curses associated with the burial sites (pyramids) of some Egyptian pharaohs, for example of the Eighteenth Dynasty, which did not deter greedy grave-robbers from digging for 'hidden treasure.'"[31] In a blasphemous way, its observations take thinking about nature back to that spiritual dimension that dwelt within it in the thought of

American and European Romanticism, and whose long shadow still touches us today when we are surprised by the concurrence of the most poisonous landscape and the greatest biodiversity.

In these cases, the idea of an untouched nature is profoundly undermined by the animals who live there, and that is surely a good thing. For the notion of an untouched nature is a deeply bourgeois idea that was put forward by the very people who could afford not to touch nature because they did not have to work in and with it. Human labour and untouched nature do not get along well in such imaginaries. Moreover, the idea of untouched nature plays humans and nature off against each other in an extreme way and is profoundly anti-urban. Cecil Konijnendijk, on the other hand, points out that two-thirds of all birds species in Germany live in the capital Berlin, while Zurich harbours ten times more foxes, hedgehogs, and badgers per square mile than the surrounding Swiss countryside: "Part of the explanation is that cities offer a mosaic of habitats and microclimates, from pond-filled gardens to industrial brownfield sites and, of course, city forests."[32]

Urban nature, radioactively contaminated no-go zones, and poison gas production plants boast a more diverse nature than many nature preserves and national parks. The latter, however, offer a territory that is often nationalistically charged, whether mountain peaks in an Austrian *Heimat* film,[33] the frontier myth of the American Wild West, or the German forest, which during the period of nationalistic Romanticism was reforested or rearranged to match ancient sources.

FROM NATURE AS PUNISHMENT TO NATURE AS REDEMPTION

Cronon stresses that until the eighteenth century untouched nature was fraught with religious images of punishment and terror. Untouched nature was the place into which Adam and Eve were cast as punishment. Untouched nature was the place where the Israelites, during their forty-year exile, began to worship a golden calf, and where Jesus was led into temptation by the Devil. You didn't go there by choice, and civilized people could not expect to find much of anything uplifting there.

Romanticism, Cronon writes, brought a new transatlantic concept of nature—that of the sublime.

> In the theories of Edmund Burke, Immanuel Kant, William Gilpin, and others, sublime landscapes were those rare places on earth where one had more chance than elsewhere to glimpse the face of God. Romantics had a clear notion of where one could be most sure of having this experience. Although God might, of course, choose to show Himself anywhere, He would most often be found in those vast, powerful landscapes where one could not help feeling insignificant and being reminded of one's own mortality. Where were these sublime places? The eighteenth-century catalog of their locations feels very familiar, for we still see and value landscapes as it taught us to do. God was on the mountaintop, in

the chasm, in the waterfall, in the thundercloud, in
the rainbow, in the sunset.[34]

In the places where one could experience these spectacles most impressively, the first national parks of the United States were established: Yellowstone, Yosemite, Grand Canyon, Rainier, Zion. But whereas in Thoreau and Burke the sublime was always something divinely unhuman, something that unleashed shudders, dread, and terror in humans, during the increasingly democratized visits to nature of late Romanticism the sublime was firmly reined in:

> As more and more tourists sought out the wilderness
> as a spectacle to be looked at and enjoyed for its great
> beauty, the sublime in effect became domesticated.
> The wilderness was still sacred, but the religious
> sentiments it evoked were more those of a pleasant
> parish church than those of a grand cathedral or a
> harsh desert retreat.[35]

Today, nature has become the place where survival skills are trained, where history hangs in the balance, where one part of it is privileged at the cost of another. Yet if talk about nature or naturalness has any meaning at all, then it is to remind us that something different or someone different from ourselves exists (at least in the way we understand and perceive ourselves at this point in time). The sewers under the Berghain are just as much nature as a small concrete pond, filled with leeches and overgrown with algae, in the neglected land around an urban housing complex. But we believe: "If it isn't hundreds of square miles big, if it doesn't give us God's-eye views or grand vistas, if it doesn't permit us the illusion that we are alone on the planet, then it really isn't natural. It's too small, too plain, or too crowded."[36]

IMPERIAL NOSTALGIA

Some of us relate to animals and nature in patronizing ways, based on rigid and ahistorical notions of what form nature should take and how animals should behave. And sometimes we allow ourselves to relate this way to fellow humans, as is especially evident in the case of "tribal people" and Indigenous societies. Associating Indigenous people with some unspoiled part of nature that exists outside of the rest of humanity reduces them to mere bearers of dubious conceptions of "authenticity." Juan José Luis Katira Ramirez, a shaman and intellectual of the Wixárika in Mexico, explains: "Foreigners often ask me whether there are still authentic 'Indians' at all, and they expect the answer that there are very few left who carry on with some of the old traditions. It is mostly the old ones who are able to recount some of the otherwise forgotten myths, and the young ones have long moved to the cities, where they inevitably assimilate."[37]

It is true that imperial powers have brought immense misery to Indigenous societies all over the world, but it is important not to miss the diverse ways in which different societies have responded or could respond.[38] For instance, the Wixárika frustrate the imperial longing for a homogenous Indigenous constellation of vanishing worlds. They reject the role attributed to them of a human version of the Western idea of pristine nature, always at the brink of disappearance, always needing to be saved by benevolent and understanding outsiders. "In the last decades health care and schooling improved, the participation in rituals and municipal assemblies intensified," Ramirez notes.

Indeed, many Wixárika drive SUVs and reside in villas, while at the same time living for several months of the year without modern amenities in order to participate in peyote ceremonies and grow corn in a sweat-inducingly traditional way (without the use of modern technologies). Many Wixárika have by no means given up their beliefs and practices, yet they seem to thrive in contemporary capitalism.[39] Their numbers are growing, they are taking on more territory, skilfully manipulating the media, and selling tourists cheap souvenirs, while keeping the precious and magical artifacts for themselves. It appears that some of us are less interested in the complex realities of Indigenous peoples, their struggles and desires, contradictions and tactics, than in confirming our own narcissistic gaze on the other.

YOUR BODY: TEMPLE OR BOUNCY CASTLE

The more polluted we feel to ourselves, the more we wish for something edifying, something pure, by which we can pull ourselves up to our full height. The way we look at our own bodies and the feelings we bring to nature are linked. Therefore the question of our own body image arises together with our view of other ecologies. Do we view our own bodies as temples to be carefully purified, as a church worthy of our reverence, or as an amusement centre, a kind of bouncy castle?

The particular attention that has been paid in recent years to smoking as an immoral activity provides an illustrative example. If you smoke, you are not only treating your own body irresponsibly, but you're also damaging the environment (children, animals, restaurant staff, bystanders)—this is the new biopolitical common sense. Current research indicates that, at least in an ecological sense, the opposite could be true: more and more birds are incorporating cigarette butts into their nests, because they not only make the nest warmer and softer, but also drastically reduce the number of ectoparasites in the nest.

Researchers working with Monserrat Suárez-Rodríguez of the Universidad Nacional Autónoma de México have studied the nests of sparrows and house finches in urban zones and discovered that in 90 percent of the nests analyzed, the birds had incorporated cigarette butts.[40] It has long been known that many bird species go out of their way to weave particular parts of plants into their nests when they are infested with mites. In this case too, the nicotine in the discarded cigarette butts presumably acts as a repellent. After all, tobacco plants also use it to ward off insects:

> The more cigarette butts a nest possessed, the fewer mites made mischief there, reported the biologists. . . . They offered a horde of mice the choice

between a dwelling made out of filters from smoked cigarettes, and an artificial nest made of "virgin" filter material. The result: the parasites avoided the smoked alternative but made themselves at home in the smoke-free nest. The bottom line is clear: the use of cigarette waste as nest material works like a pest control measure, say the researchers.[41]

For too long, order-loving eco-police have presented nature as a well-trimmed garden of human moral tastes. The nest-building habits of Mexican birds and the hormone-drenched songs of British birds run counter to the control fantasies of eco-morally pure spaces and bio-morally pure bodies.

CLOUDY SWORDS

So let us thank this small insect, the mosquito, which has preserved the land of our ancestors for us.
—Sanja Doyo Onabamiro, Ibadan, Nigeria[1]

The honeybee has recently risen to become the "insect mascot of environmental politics"[2] and has outstripped the save the whale and dolphin campaigns of the 1970s and 1980s. Whereas French environmental activists who publicly placed a beehive on the roof of the Paris Opera were immediately arrested, today it seems there is hardly a major cultural institution in the big cities of the West that doesn't point proudly to an urban beehive on its roof.

The fruit of the labour of the industrious female insects can then usually be purchased onsite in containers smartly designed by local or international artists. In the museum gift shops, the proverbial *busyness* of the bees combines with the creativity of the artists into the effective public relations of a creative industries appeal under the banner of commercialized sustainability and ecological diversity.

The honeybee is a darling animal of ecocapitalists not only because it links worry about survival on the planet with agricultural interests, but also because it carries substantial metaphorical baggage as a hardworking producer, organized on the basis of division of labour, of medically valuable luxury comestibles and nutritious foods, all while connecting big cities with global ecology. Nowadays bees are prized by an increasing number of newcomers to the field of beekeeping "as trendy urban pets to be nurtured and rescued."[3]

The honeybee has little to do with nature in the traditional sense. As a rule we are talking about breeding lines that are kept in rationalized Langstroth hives named after the American beekeeper and clergyman Lorenzo L. Langstroth. Langstroth had further developed the concept of modern, efficient beekeeping proposed by the Swiss beekeeper François Huber. Not long after Jeremy Bentham had presented his first designs for a panopticon that modernized the visual surveillance of prison inmates, Huber's rationalized beehives made it possible to inspect bees effortlessly. They consisted of square wooden frames with identical dimensions that could be "opened" like the pages of a book.[4] Now nothing could escape the scrutinizing gaze: what was ready to harvest, what was sick and needed to be culled, and what could be left in place to thrive on its own.

READING MATERIAL FOR THE ROAD TO HELL

Bees are by no means innocent representatives of nature. The commonly known honeybee (*Apis mellifera*) was introduced to North America by European settlers, and spread as quickly as the white settler families. Since bees swarm out on their own, they formed a colonial avant garde that flew fifty to a hundred kilometres ahead of the advancing frontier of colonization, which was not lost on the Indigenous nations.[5] It is part of the political poetry of Jim Jarmusch's anti-Western *Dead Man* (1995), probably the most artistically precise reckoning with the historic and cinematic founding myth of the United States, that even this detail is seen more sharply than by most others. In the film's opening sequence, Johnny Depp, playing an accountant from Cleveland named William Blake, is sitting on a train on his way take up a job offer in a city called Machine. Along with the train (an old symbol of progress and industrialization) he reenacts the historical expansion westward. During the trip the other passengers become more and more frightening and desolate, appearing "jagged, ragged, disheveled and uncivilized."[6]

At one point they jump up and shoot wildly out of the window—"murderous fun," killing bison by the hundreds; later a stoker, who seems to have sprung right out of a Kafka novel, sits down by the timid Blake and asks him what motivated him to set off on the road to hell. For a few seconds, hell is visible in the form of a burned-down Indigenous village. Blake quickly turns his attention back to the magazine he has chosen as his travelling companion on his road to hell. The magazine is titled *The Illustrated Bee Journal.* Now, for a few seconds, advertisements for products like "Vandalia" can be seen: civilization and barbarism switch places. If the Vandals once sacked Rome, it is now the Romans, as the real barbarians, who are ransacking the Vandals.

IMPERIAL INSECTS

Today bees are deliberately incorporated into neocolonial pacification strategies. The US Armed Forces research network is testing the deployment of bees as "six-legged soldiers,"[7] which in the coming wars will be "efficient and effective homeland security detective devices,"[8] designed to detect insurgents' bombs more cheaply and quickly than ever before, at least according to a report from the Stealthy Insect Sensor project team at the Los Alamos National Laboratory.[9]

While the female worker bees perform a variety of jobs in the hive, the male drones are limited to very specific tasks. Mary Kosut and Lisa Jean Moore draw the metaphorical lines of connection between beekeeping and modern military policy in the figure of the "specialized, specific, and covert" work of predator drones as they have been routinely deployed by the US military since the presidency of Barack Obama for the extrajudicial execution of those designated as "enemy combatants": "in both bee culture and military culture, the role of drones is reduced to the performance of a series of 'heroic' duties [, namely,] surveillance, bomb dropping, and insemination."[10]

But anyone who survives the drone attacks is still not spared from metaphorical and real insects, for insects are a part of the "war on terror," as was revealed in 2009 by the publication of CIA memos on permissible torture techniques. Second to last on the list of ten "legitimate" torture techniques, between "sleep deprivation" and "waterboarding," is "insects placed in a detention box."[11] The unredacted part of the memo explains that Abu Zubaydah (who was apprehended in Pakistan in 2002 and then moved through a chain of offshore CIA prisons in Thailand, Poland, and Jordan, until he landed in Guantanamo for an indefinite stay) was physically and mentally so strong that normal interrogation techniques no longer worked. Therefore, his fear of insects was to be instrumentalized in the cause of national defence. According to the memo, the plan was to lock Abu Zubaydah in a cramped box (the eighteen-hour box permits only standing and the two-hour box only sitting) and to tell him that a stinging insect would be placed in it. But the actual plan was to use a harmless caterpillar.[12] Without giving any rationale, the memorandum explains that this specific torture technique was no longer used. Nonetheless, the imaginary insect remained a state secret until 2009.[13]

Neel Ahuja argues that this seemingly subtle technique for producing truth through "bestial touch"[14] follows a liberal logic that measures how humane and civilized torture by "trans-species intimacy" is in terms of the alleged absence of permanent physical and psychological damage.[15] For Ahuja, the meaning of this well-calculated abandonment of an apparently unusual torture method by the highest levels of the US government is only explicable when one considers a broader discursive semantic landscape that comprises the current racialization of the "brown Muslim multitude," colonial rhetoric, the insectoid imagination of terrorist forms of action and communication, as well as gendered bodies and "weaponized affects": "Following the double structure of metaphoric relations of insects to the terrorist psyche, the insect is both the weapon against an enemy and a description of that animalized enemy; the monster-terrorist is an insect that must be squashed, paradoxically by the threat of insectity to his masculine self-image."[16]

MOSQUITO ARMY

While bees are currently esteemed as universally valued bringers of life, there is another insect that can't be left off of any Buzzfeed listicle of the world's deadliest animals: the mosquito. No other animal accounts for as many human fatalities as this insect. That's why the eradication of mosquitoes is a typical focus of philanthropic initiatives, from the Rockefeller Foundation to the Bill & Melinda Gates Foundation. But what if the front lines are not so clear-cut?

The term "differential immunity" describes the phenomenon that people who have contracted malaria, for instance, early in life and survived have an advantage if reinfected over those who are fighting it for the first time. This influenced colonial entanglements and struggles for national independence, as the historian John McNeill argues.

For example, when the Maroons of Suriname were gripped by revolutionary fever in the 1770s, malarial fever swept away the Dutch punitive force. McNeill waggishly demands a monument to mosquitoes next to the stone presidents on Mount Rushmore, because the American Revolution would also have had a different outcome if the anticolonial forces had not had an advantage over the British pacification troops because of their prior immunity.[17]

In fact, the often fatal fevers known as malaria were recognized as the greatest health hazard for Europeans in tropical areas, and considered a major obstacle to the further colonization of territories beyond the coastal areas of Africa, South America, and Asia. Colonial military analysts regarded malaria "as an already existing enemy resisting imperial expansion."[18] Yet only at the end of the eighteenth century did this battle between malaria and militarism reach its peak, as the anthropologist Diane Nelson explains:

> The creation of transportation infrastructure such as canals and railroads, the deployment of armies, and the clearing of ground to plant tropical products all had to confront (in addition to uprisings, escape, work slowdowns, and other human-level obstacles) an invisible microbial resistance. The French, British, and US raced to find a cure for malaria in order to keep whites alive in their new milieux.[19]

One French colonial official complained in 1908: "fever and dysentery are the 'generals' that defend hot countries against our incursions and prevent us from replacing the aborigines that we have to make use of."[20] While infectious diseases were the generals of the anticolonial resistance, tropical medicine was assigned the role of a "counterinsurgent field."[21]

It comes as little surprise that the most important researchers in this field were officers serving in colonial outposts. In 1897 in Calcutta, this transimperial medical-military network (which was supported by countless local helpers) finally succeeded in scientifically proving the "mosquito theory": mosquitoes were identified as carriers of the malaria pathogen from infected to non-infected persons.[22] The shift toward Pasteur's microbial theory as a key to understanding diseases "structured a powerful imaginary of the colonies as vast laboratories where the enactment of hygienic measures could be tested, and the results compared across time and space."[23] Until then, prevailing theories in tropical medicine had attributed the fever to noxious vapours issuing from the ground (hence the name *mal'aria*, "bad air"). "Once germ theory was recognized, the idea of 'environment' became internalized and miniaturized in the form of invading entities; the key to medical success was now to exert control over body invaders."[24]

THE BIRTH OF SEGREGATION FROM THE SPIRIT OF MOSQUITO CONTROL

Humans living in imperial spheres of influence were suddenly brought into focus as a medically dangerous part of this environment: the Colonial Office promptly sent an expedition into the most malaria-infested corners of the British Empire. As the main problem, they quickly identified the African child. While adult Africans exhibited only mild malaria symptoms, African children often got seriously ill. Now that colonial medicine had defined them as the main reservoir of pathogenic germs, the expedition concluded its final report with the urgent recommendation to isolate white settlers and officials from African children. The suggestion was accepted. But how wide should the isolation zone be to guarantee that no bloodthirsty female mosquito could overcome it in her search for a drop of blood?

It was agreed that all new European settlements were to be surrounded by an anti-mosquito zone with no dwellings approximately four hundred metres wide, and that no locals were allowed to live within this area, so as to prevent female mosquitoes from feasting on infected children and then biting a European. Secondly, the exclusion belts were intended to provide protection from bush fires, which were allegedly especially common in the locals' neighbourhoods, and thirdly they were supposed to protect the Europeans from "having their rest disturbed by drumming or other noises dear to the Natives."[25] Emma Umana Clasberry points out that this form of segregation was even implemented in regions of Nigeria that were hardly affected by bush fires. Nor was segregation restricted to residential areas: "Even cemeteries were segregated."[26]

Since mosquitoes are nocturnal creatures, segregation had to be most strictly enforced at night. While officials and merchants performed their duties during the day in the city, during the dangerous African nights they were protected from children and mosquitoes in their gated communities. But because Europeans also didn't want to give up the amenities that made the colonies so attractive, i.e., servants, they were permitted to continue housing two servants for personal services in remote rooms at the back of the house, which undermined all of the segregationist health efforts.[27]

The segregationist mosquito doctrine was administered in Africa with varying degrees of strictness: from its most stringent form in the Belgian Congo, where the *cordon sanitaire* included a golf course, a botanical garden, and a zoo; to West Africa, where in the new city of Dakar, after the malaria outbreak of 1914 all traditional attic houses in the European residential neighbourhoods were burned down; to the German colony Cameroon, where in 1904 the medical authorities published a city map that suggested dividing the city into six areas on the basis of race and race mixture.[28]

In Accra, the capital of Ghana, European merchants were permitted to work near the harbour during the day. But they were legally required to spend the nights half a mile away in a European "reservation"—"a distance that was farther than a mosquito flight."[29]

To gain more precise data about the flight behaviour and biting patterns of the mosquitoes, migrant men were quartered in mosquito traps along the protection zone around the airport and prohibited from leaving the traps at night.[30] When it turned out that female mosquitoes could fly about one mile, the village of Nima was suddenly within the protection zone and was relocated, that is, its inhabitants were evacuated—it is not known under what circumstances.[31]

In South Africa, the hill stations became part of the "clean air circuit" that attracted many sick and debilitated Europeans from the overcrowded cities of the old continent to regain their health in the colonies before travelling back to carry out their duties at home. At the same time, hill stations and the European "healthy quarters" finally allowed familial reunification for civil servants who had left their families in their country of origin to work in the colonies—a process that helped end decades of racial mixing and personal relationships on various levels.[32]

The colonial city planning policy of using the range of movement of female mosquitoes to determine where exactly the local population was allowed to live lasted about ten years and had passed its peak by 1920. Responsible for its demise were the local elites, who put pressure on the British colonial officials from Hong Kong to India: "Their arguments against the expropriation of their lands for the health needs of a handful of Europeans—who then proceeded to live with lower class African servants, mistresses, and sometimes their mistresses' supposedly deadly children—were even persuasive to colonial governors."[33]

The policy of segregation for health reasons was abandoned, at least rhetorically—after all, the cities were already built—but many of the models of segregated urban residential areas that had been implemented persisted well beyond this time.[34] We have the fight against the mosquito to thank for one of the worst ideas in the political history of social relations: segregation. The concept originally arose in the medical field and meant the isolation of "contagious" *individuals*. The first time the expression was used to denote a spatial separation of a general *group* was in a 1904 issue of the *British Medical Journal*: "Manson has also declared segregation to be the first law of hygiene for Europeans in the tropics."[35] As a "class term, it soon became, in South Africa, America, and elsewhere, a key word in the vocabulary of race relations in the twentieth century."[36]

WOMEN IN PANAMA

At the beginning of the twentieth century, the discovery of mosquitoes as malaria and yellow fever carriers reawakened long-cherished plans such as the construction of the Panama Canal (1904–1914), which was to link the Atlantic and Pacific Oceans. Finally, a majority of the workers employed no longer constantly got sick or died.[37]

In 1916, the director of the US Bureau of Entomology and longtime general secretary of the American Association for the Advancement of Science rejoiced at this success as "an object lesson for the sanitarians of the world"—it demonstrated "that it is possible for the white race to live healthfully in the tropics."[38] As Timothy Mitchell writes: "In 1915, the year after the canal's completion, the newly established Rockefeller Foundation took over the mosquito campaign from the U.S. army and launched a worldwide program to study and control the two mosquito-borne diseases. Thus the global movements of the mosquito gave shape to a transnational corporate philanthropy."[39] Disease was to be defeated not by improving social conditions or through medical intervention, but by the physical elimination of the hostile species. For the first time, war was declared on the mosquito.[40]

The urgency and severity of measures to combat dangerous diseases always had the collateral benefit of social pacification. In 1918, George Vincent, president of the Rockefeller Foundation, candidly declared: "For purposes of placating primitive and suspicious peoples, medicine has some decided advantages over machine guns."[41]

The construction of the Panama Canal, as one of the most important "transportation utopias" of the twentieth century, not only allowed commodities to be shipped more efficiently and quickly, but it also advanced the military expansion of the United States in the Caribbean.[42] The US occupation of the Canal Zone had already brought racist Jim Crow laws, which had followed the abolition of slavery in the US, to the spatial structure around the canal. Yet, when the increasing presence of US troops and the flow of migrant labourers in the Canal Zone during the two world wars heightened fears of sexually transmitted diseases, "a medicalized state of war . . . attacked environmental space using the model of antimalarial campaigns aimed at controlling mosquitoes."[43]

Analogous to the stagnant waters where mosquito larvae develop, and to the mosquitoes themselves, the female body was now declared to be a reservoir of pathogens. Again and again, this body allegedly first infected US troops, only to spread to the white wives back home: "The spatial imaginary established through control of malarial mosquitoes deeply influenced cartographies" of sexually transmitted diseases like gonorrhea and syphilis, as well as the attempt to control them.[44] Although US troops themselves were an excellent vehicle for the global spread of disease, the risk was one-sidedly shifted to the local population and migrant workers, "conflating the body of the sex worker with the US occupation itself."[45]

Besides the inspection and closing of brothels and the establishment and expansion of vice squads and prophylaxis stations, during the night women were picked up all over the city and forcibly tested for sexually transmitted diseases—if the results were positive, they were detained in something between a prison and hospital for up to six months. This control over the movement of women in public spaces as potential sex workers and disease reservoirs was carried out just as women's rights activists were increasingly drawing attention to themselves in the 1940s.[46]

FASCISM AND THE GODDESS OF FEVER

At the same time women in Panama were becoming objects of police surveillance by way of combatting malaria, Italian fascism was trying to defeat a nature imagined as female by declaring it a priority to civilize the marshes of the Pontine Plain. The ancient Roman rhetorician Cicero had already described this landscape southeast of Rome as "neither pleasant nor healthy." This had hardly changed in two thousand years. The swampland was still the habitat of the anopheles mosquito and the dominion of the "Goddess of Fever."[47]

In Italian fascism, malaria seemed to be a flaw of a primal, feminine, sterile nature, whose unproductive development was to be prevented through the use of technology and science, chemistry, and propaganda, turning it into a second state of nature: "The mosquito was taken by the fascists to exemplify the evil character of pre-fascist nature in the marshes." The efforts to create "an idyllic rural area consonant with fascist ideals of productivity and activity within the state's interests"[48] included extensive electrification of the region, constructing thousands of kilometres of roads and canals and "large pumping and drainage plants called *impianti idrovori* (drainage pumping stations), in Italian literally 'water-eating' machinery plants," founding an anti-malaria institute, having war veterans plant the region with water-absorbing eucalyptus trees (these plants performed their job too well, which is why they were later torn out again at great expense—as a consequence, there are about four tornadoes annually in this area), stocking fish to eat mosquito larvae, establishing an anti-mosquito militia, and putting up children's camps whose buildings were wrapped in ten layers of wire to protect them from mosquitoes. "The fascist emphasis on the technical and technological aspects of the land reclamation programme were also characteristic of a positivistic view of science and geographical knowledge, aimed at controlling, rationalizing and ultimately creating an imperium over a previously unknown or 'untamed' area."[49]

TOXIC PROGRESS

At the same time in the Pacific, in spite of all countermeasures, malaria was inflicting more fatalities on the Allies than the Japanese forces were. But the discovery of a potent molecule brought new momentum to the anti-malaria campaigns: "From the perspective of medical entomology, the most exciting outcome of World War II was the discovery of DDT."[50]

Dichloro-diphenyl-trichlorethane had already been synthesized in Germany in the 1870s, but it was only in the last years of the war that people became aware of a special quality of DDT. The molecule not only killed mosquito larvae in water, but even months after a surface had been treated with it, it was still lethal to any mosquito that landed on it.

Once again, the Rockefeller Foundation became active, and together with the World Health Organization, the US Agency for International Development, and the UN, it launched the Global Malaria Eradication Program, which coordinated the worldwide deployment of DDT in the 1950s and 1960s, with the goal of eliminating malaria. This deadly substance became part of a postwar order that organized war and agriculture as affiliated fields: "Tractors and tanks developed side by side. Synthetic nitrogen fertilizers were manufactured cheaply in ammonia plants built mainly to produce nitrate explosives. Modern organic insecticides emerged from gas weapon research between the wars, while aerial spraying owes much to air combat methods and technology initially developed during World War I."[51]

In the Global Malaria Eradication Program, health and chemistry became essential parts of a technocratic vision of modernity that lined up cold warriors and warm habitats on the battlefield. In the context of decolonization movements and nation building after World War II, the female mosquito was declared an enemy of the state: in Peronist Argentina a state of emergency was declared in the fight against mosquitoes in order to use violent police enforcement to fog even the last slum hut with DDT.[52] And probably the first international act of the Egyptian president Nasser, who had just come to power in 1952, was to sign an agreement with the WHO and UNICEF to establish a DDT factory near Kafr Zayat "that would produce two hundred tons a year of finished DDT."[53]

The staging of nation-building and anti-malaria campaigns often had militaristic features: in 1955, a large Indian newspaper reported that the Ahmedabad Corporation had sprayed seven thousand tenements in working-class neighbourhoods with DDT on the occasion of World Health Week. In Shillong, in northeastern India, and in southern Hyderabad, mass demonstrations were organized by doctors and nurses who carried posters reading "Lead Healthy Lives and Keep Your Surroundings Clean." Meanwhile, two aircraft from the Indian Air Force rained health brochures down on the population in Hyderabad and Secunderabad—only seven years after Hyderabad had been forcibly incorporated into the new Indian state. This was both a promise of future health and a powerful assurance that come what may, it would happen in the state that had been established.[54]

At the same time, there were increasing reports about disastrous effects of the global field trials of chemical insecticides. In hindsight, the military policy of eradication turned out not only to be futile and counterproductive (the absolute and relative number of malaria infections is globally higher than before the start of the eradication campaign), but with the publication of Rachel Carson's *Silent Spring* (1962), which portrayed the effects of the poison on bird populations, it also promoted the emergence of the ecological movement in the West and led to the banning of DDT in the United States. For in spite of initial successes, DDT-resistant mosquitoes quickly developed, first in Sardinia, and then in Greece, where DDT had been widely used. In the 1960s and 1970s, malaria reappeared in many places and the idea that malaria could be eliminated was postponed to some distant future.

"Since the 1990s the post-eradication era has been interpreted as a time of total confusion, even of anarchy,"[55] since opinions on what, if anything, might be learned from this period differ widely. According to the anthropologist David Turnbull, a major reason for this confusion lies in the fact that malaria is a case of *motley*, a patchwork or crazy-quilt, a term historically used to describe the piebald costumes of jesters or "motley fools." To think of malaria as a "motley" means to understand this phenomenon as "a ragbag of different strains of the parasite and of interacting processes"[56]—not as a disease that can be attributed to the mere presence of a foreign species in the human body.

Turnbull enumerates various conceptualizations of malaria during the twentieth century: malaria was seen as a political, administrative, social, technical, economic, or ecological problem, whereas in Papua New Guinea, coastal dwellers reserved the Tok Pisin expression "samting nating" (something nothing) for it, and malariologists in the United States, after all attempts at producing a vaccine failed, declared in tautological exasperation that malaria is anything that reacts to anti-malarial drugs.[57]

What exactly reacts to anti-malarial drugs remains indefinite and potentially dangerous, but this doesn't keep armies or pharmaceutical companies from repeatedly promising and administering "safe" preventive drugs. In 2002 there were reports of rampages by four American war veterans who had just returned home to North Carolina from Afghanistan and each independently murdered their wives (one had seventy-one knife wounds). All four of them had taken Lariam (mefloquine) to prevent malaria. Lariam was developed jointly by the Walter Reed Army Institute of Research (WRAIR), the US Army, and the pharmaceutical company F. Hoffmann-La Roche AG. Lariam—it is not known exactly how it works—is associated with severe neuropsychiatric disorders including manic behaviour, acute psychosis with delusions, and aggressive mood swings, and so suspicion quickly fell on the drug.[58] Diane Nelson points out that an official army report cleared the drug of any suspicion just in time for it to be distributed to 200,000 soldiers in Iraq: "Little mention was made of military training itself as a lethal drug or of the way that soldiers' willingness to die has made them excellent guinea pigs in military laboratories, where unapproved drugs are routinely tested."[59]

IMPERIAL, COLONIAL, NATIONAL, NGO

The history of the struggle against the female mosquito reads like the history of capitalism in the twentieth century: after imperial, colonial, and nationalistic periods of combatting mosquitoes, we are now in the NGO phase, characterized by shrinking government health care budgets, privatization through structural adjustment programs, and intensified activity on the part of non-governmental organizations and development agencies. The Rockefeller Foundation was once again at the forefront when in 2018 the Bill & Melinda Gates Foundation declared it was investing $3.4 million in the development of genetically modified male mosquitoes. When they are released in large numbers, all their offspring will die after one mating—at least that's the plan. Mosquitoes don't transmit malaria anymore, they are turned into agents of health: "GM mosquitoes render the mosquitoes themselves as a commercial product; a commercial product in a political economy funded by philanthropic initiatives, shaped by private university spin-offs and characterized through economic inequalities."[60]

It is still unclear what consequences this new strategy of releasing insectoid reproduction bombs will have, but the effects of the latest global campaign of the NGO phase are already making themselves felt. Charitable initiatives committed to the free distribution of insecticide-impregnated mosquito nets have led to an economic redistribution from local producers of traditional mosquito nets to industrial sites in Vietnam and Thailand that are capable of producing huge quantities of insecticide-treated nets.[61]

A study of the effects of these modern mosquito nets in Ghana shows that after an initial improvement, the situation could get considerably worse: the main effect of the impregnated nets is not keeping mosquitoes away from people (traditional nets could do this just as well), but that contact with the net is fatal to the mosquitoes, and also that mosquitoes are deterred from getting near the net, since the chemicals have a repellent effect. In other words: the impregnation with insecticide produces a second biochemical net that is greater than the textile net itself. This results in an immense pressure to adapt: first, normal mosquitoes die in great numbers or are kept from moving near the nets. Within the mosquito population, however, more and more subpopulations emerge that react with altered behaviour: largely avoiding interior spaces and swarming out earlier, which means that even non-impregnated nets lose their effectiveness and the number of infections increasingly grows higher than before the distribution of the free nets.

For the anthropologist Uli Beisel, the recalcitrance of mosquitoes toward the charitable efforts to control them shows on the one hand in the mosquitoes' altered behaviour described above, and on the other hand physically, in the form of the mosquitoes' increasing tolerance for insecticides. The latter occurs first through mutations in precisely those parts of the insects' nervous systems that are targeted by the toxins, and secondly through metabolic changes that render the toxins harmless before they reach their target, and thirdly by the adaptation of the mosquito's cuticle, through which the toxin is absorbed. Chemical similarities between the indoor anti-mosquito toxins (nets and aerosols) and those used in agriculture lead to cross-immunizations that reinforce the new resistance.[62]

If animals in modernity functioned as humans' other (nature, instinct, wildness, lack of speech, lack of history, lack of a soul, and so on), insects are the other of animals. Insects seem to possess no form of individuality; they don't even have a face from which we could read expressions of an inner life. Declaring humans to be insects is therefore the most radical form of dehumanization.

In Western modernity, dealing with unpleasant and potentially deadly insects has usually taken on the form of a military confrontation bent on annihilation. Uli Beisel's proposal for a ceasefire therefore seems provocative: "What if managing mosquitoes is not about how to best eliminate them, but about asking how we might find ways to tolerate coexisting with each other?"[63]

THE HAMBURG TERMITES

Whereas the battle against mosquitoes was part of colonial expansion strategies, in the twentieth century another insect set out to colonize the colonizers themselves. We are talking about the termite, whose conquest of a northern German city also shook certainties about which animal belongs where.

When in the eighteenth century Africa was being mapped and explored by an army of scientists, the colonialists were forced to realize—what a surprise!—that Africa had already been colonized: by white ants, as termites were originally called. Later, legions of ethnographic photographs showed seemingly primitive people and their huts next to the elaborate architecture of these other Africans, which by comparison resembled high-rises of unimaginable height, leaving European engineers in a state of perplexed envy.[64]

It was probably shortly after the German Empire had carried out a campaign of racist collective punishment against the Herero and Nama peoples in the colony of German South West Africa (today Namibia) in the early twentieth century that the colonizers themselves were colonized—by termites.[65]

The "destructive, wood-munching creatures"[66] had in all probability made it to Hamburg with imported wood that was used for the cladding of the new Hamburg heating system. The termites would probably not have survived a single winter in the cold climate of northern Europe, but luckily for them, in 1921 the local electric company had begun to channel waste heat from the generation of electricity through a pipe system to government offices and homes.[67] The implementation of a district heating grid under the city also offered the termites a solution to the problem of the cold northern European climate: "The barely insulated pipes warmed the earth, the wood was delicious—all was well with the termites."[68]

The other problem—the wood being too dry for the termites' purposes—was solved by the animals themselves, by constructing mud tubes in the ground. This supplied the colony with the moisture necessary to keep the thin skins and soft bodies of its members from drying out. With thousands of hungry mouths, the termite colony henceforth chewed its way through subterranean Hamburg and crisscrossed the open spaces in protective tunnels.

In all probability, the termites were living in a thriving colony when they were discovered in 1937. A construction worker had put his jacket on a pile of wood near the entrance to the district heating network—only to watch as the pile turned into a heap of sawdust.

The heating ducts were not only an ideal winter home for the termites, they also served as underground guide rails for the colonization of the city: the termites followed the duct grid and worked their way up to the trees of the Karolinenviertel district ("Karoviertel") and the Justice Forum, where they still live to this day.

While the Karoviertel was being overrun by a congenial

army of creative types and becoming a trendy residential neighbourhood with all of the well-known problems of gentrification, at the same time the venerable Justice Forum (consisting of the Higher Regional Court, and the Criminal Justice and Civil Justice buildings) was being attacked from below. One city official reports that the worst nightmare of all property owners became reality when civil servants discovered that the termites had started to devour the state registry records—thousands of tiny Bakunins.[69]

It had been the strategic goal of all Bakunin-style anarchist revolts to destroy as many local records of deed registries and bank liabilities as possible before normal class rule could be restored. Ironically, a contemporary anti-termite poison is being marketed by BASF under the brand name Termidor, which unintentionally draws a connection to Leon Trotsky's coinage of the term "Thermidor" for the counterrevolutionary phase of the bureaucratic restoration of power.[70] In the corporate Newspeak presented to us on the Termidor company website, control means killing, design is extermination, and lifetime is a registered trademark: "For the best termite control solution, turn to Termidor® ... as seen on Designing Spaces on Lifetime®."[71]

The files were quickly relocated, but even after a series of countermeasures over the past ninety years, including the subterranean installation of glass barricades and the massive deployment of heat to dry them out, the termites are still a problem. Even the removal of entire houses and experimental hormone therapy by a research unit of the German armed forces did little to help.[72]

The old tactics of mass poisoning of entire districts with

highly toxic substances and introducing of all kinds of insecticides into bricks and wood were common into the 1980s, but the latest weapon is intelligent poisoning by means of "homeopathic doses" of lethal substances—in concentrations low enough to be carried back to the colony and fed to the other termites, so that the poison can accumulate over time and unleash its effect. According to official estimates, in certain parts of the city 95 percent of Hamburg's termite population was killed, but in the meantime new areas have been colonized. Children are warned in German teaching materials: "Success is always in danger: sometimes the termites don't like the taste of the bait, sometimes a termite-free zone is re-infested."[73]

NATIONAL ECHOES

Even though the termites have certainly cost the city and its homeowners a considerable sum of money, termite species have only recently been scientifically defined as "invasive," with only 27 of 2,750 described termite species falling into this category, and trade in goods is the single most important factor in their spread.[74] The invasiveness of biological species only seems obvious; actually, it not easy to observe. Moreover, the research field of invasion ecology was not established until 1958, and it has the reputation of being especially "jargon-rich."[75] This means that the terms used are often not precisely defined or generally accepted.

The historically controversial problem of invasiveness is closely bound up with the concept of habitat. But what is a habitat? "Habitat" describes a spatial unity between individuals and species: the space that a particular population needs to be able to reproduce. The term was first used in Carl von Linné's *Systema Naturae* (1758). But whereas the Latin word *habitat* simply means "he/she/it lives" or "he/she/it dwells" and was originally used as a verb, and thus for an activity, the term later ossified and took on the meaning of a specific spatial territory. In this new form, it could then be pervaded or conquered by "alien, adventive, exotic, foreign, non-indigenous, non-native and novel"[76] organisms. Habitat became a concept reminiscent of the idea of nations with fixed, stable, and controlled borders.

Precisely the seemingly innocent question of where which animal lives and should live cannot be separated from farther-reaching discourses of political history within which these questions are asked and answered. Science studies scholar Donna Haraway investigated the history of ideas of the immune system in the Cold War era.[77] The parallels between the conceptualization of microscopic and geopolitical models and metaphors are striking. The scientific ideas of the immune system seem to have been lifted from a NATO mission statement: the now passionately pursued definition of inside and outside seems to be as much a part of the self-protection of bodies and associations of states as does the identification and disarming of external infiltrators and internal sources of danger (like sleeper cells) that could mutate at any time from a harmless twilight state into a life-threatening proliferation. Similarly, the rhetoric of natural habitats and invasive species recalls the exiled revolutionary and cultural theorist Leon Trotsky's lament about the "planet without a visa,"[78] a dubious human privilege that is extended to the non-human world.

The dedicated efforts against the Hamburg termites cannot be reduced to purely rational discourses or practices. The problem with Hamburg's termites is that they also invade our dreams.

In his *Insectopedia* (2010), Hugh Raffles remarks that "insects are without number and without end" and the nightmares that they inhabit seem to be as numerous as the insects themselves. There are nightmares of "fertility" and of the "crowd," of "uncontrolled bodies," of "unguarded openings" and "vulnerable places," of "foreign bodies in our bloodstream" and of "foreign bodies in our ears and our eyes and under the surface of our skin." Let us not forget the "nightmare of swarming and the nightmare of crawling," the "nightmare of beings without reason and the nightmare of the inability to communicate," as well as the nightmare of "not seeing the face," and "not having a face"; it is the nightmare "of being overrun," of "being occupied," and of "being alone," of "putting on shoes" and "taking off shoes," the nightmare of "the grotesque," of the "snarled hair" and "the open mouth," the nightmare of "randomness and the unguarded moment," the nightmare

> of the military that funds nearly all basic research in insect science, the nightmare of probes into brains and razors into eyes, the nightmare that should any of this reveal the secrets of locusts swarming, of bees navigating, or of ants foraging, the secrets will beget

other secrets, the nightmares other nightmares, the
pupae other pupae, insects born of microimplants;
part-machine, part-insect insects; remote-controlled
weaponized surveillance insects; moths on a mission;
beetles undercover; not to mention robotic insects,
mass-produced, mass-deployed, mass-suicide nightmare insects. These are the nightmares that dream of
coming wars . . . dreams of Osama bin Laden somewhere in a cave.[79]

As real, symbolic, and affective agents, the Hamburg termites cause a discomfort that is like a "cloud shaped like a sword" stuck in the heart of the city. If mosquitoes *speak* through the social noise they make, as Timothy Mitchell argues in his analysis of malaria outbreaks in colonial Egypt,[80] and if tsetse flies *scream*, as Clapperton Mavhunga states in connection with the human and non-human entanglements in Zimbabwe's Gonarezhou National Park[81]—then the Hamburg termites make bambule (go on a rampage).[82]

POLITICAL SALVATION IN THE TERMITE GUT

When the termites arrived in Hamburg, the discourse around the insect had already morphed from admiration to disgust. Research had shown that termites have two stomachs—one of them being a social stomach that was emptied for other termites in the colonies. Termites that had died were also consumed. On top of that, every fellow member of the species in the colony that asked for it was given excrement to redigest. The termite colony didn't waste anything: "From behind and in front, the food continues to flow through the whole state, the returnee gives it to the one that stays at home, the old give it to the young, in an endless cycle of soup, even if the soup may be a little strange."[83] While nowadays research projects compete in learning from the sophisticated air conditioning systems of termite hills, a look inside the working of the colony offers a glimpse into the nightmare of total recycling.

The Belgian Nobel Prize winner and essayist Maurice Maeterlinck vividly described this astounding social metabolism in his *Life of the Termites* (1926): "You see, this is perfect communism, communism of the pharynx and intestines, driven by the collectivism of shit-eating. Nothing is lost in this dreary and thriving republic, where the dirty ideal that nature seems to offer us is made real in economic terms."[84]

The forestry scientist and zoologist Karl Escherich, a staunch National Socialist, picked up this thread in his inaugural address as the newly appointed rector of the University of Munich in 1933. His speech, titled "Termite Delusion," contrasted the supposedly good ant colony of the Third Reich with the diabolical termite system of the Soviet Union.[85]

In the same year in which Escherich gave his inaugural speech, another biologist, Jean L. Sutherland, published an article describing a disturbing microorganism that lived in the rectum of the Australian termite species *Mastotermes darwiniensis*.[86] Sutherland called the tiny animal *Mixotricha paradoxa*, which means "strange creature with tousled hair." While Escherich's demonization of termites because of their intestinal tract is now only of historical interest, Sutherland's discovery has been enjoying renewed attention in the past few years. The remarkable thing about *M. paradoxa* is its constitution as an organism combining four other creatures that live in and on it.

You have to picture *M. paradoxa* as a sort of hairy pear with several antennae sticking out of its head—the hair and the antennae each possess their own genome, while inside the cells of *M. paradoxa* there are two further distinct genomes. Therefore *M. paradoxa* does not have one genome, but a total of five.

Donna Haraway summarizes what it means to understand the micro-organism as a living metaphor:

> This little filamentous creature makes a mockery of the notion of the bounded, defended, singular self out to protect its genetic investments.... What constitutes *M. paradoxa*? Where does the protist stop and somebody else start in that insect's teeming hindgut? And what does this paradoxical individuality tell us about beginnings? Finally, how might such forms of life help us imagine a usable language?[87]

Is *Mixotricha paradoxa* one living being, five, or 250,000? Did it start off alone and then assimilate the other beings, or was it the one that was colonized? What was it before it became many, or vice versa: What were they before they became one? In times when social questions are being increasingly racialized and culturalized, "this tiny organism engenders key questions about the autonomy of identity."[88] Of course, there is the danger of a "biological exuberance," of trying to discern too much subversive potential in "nature's rainbow,"[89] but there may still be something to learn here. Microorganisms also account for at least half of the number of all cells in the human body. In the documentary *Golden Genes* (Konrad/Hansbauer/Stachel, 2016), the microbiologist Christa Schleper explains: "In terms of biomass, that makes up about one and a half kilograms. . . . Then the question naturally arises: What is the human? Is that *Homo sapiens* plus many bacteria? That's why people like to say that we are some kind of super organism."

Following Haraway, in the play *Das purpurne Muttermal* (The Purple Birthmark, 2006), the German dramatist René Pollesch urges us to look for new answers to problems of nationalism and identity politics in the termite piles of the world, when old answers seem to work less and less.[90] But maybe everything is even more political than we ever thought. We could be unknowingly celebrating microscopic slave labour, as philosopher and author Rupert Glasgow makes us aware:

> Consider the case of the large protozoan *Mixotricha paradoxa*, which is propelled through its environment by the coordinated undulation of what appear to be thousands of "cilia" or hair-like appendages; these appendages have been shown to be hundreds of thousands of tiny spirochaete bacteria, which—like "galley slaves"—are held in place at the cell surface by yet other bacteria.[91]

Bees, mosquitoes, and termites were not only a part of historical and contemporary notions of space, but also instruments of political practice related to spaces. As a part of the colonization of the territory that is now the United States, the honeybee was an invasive species; thanks to the global movement of goods, the termite has recently become one in Germany as well. Mosquitoes, on the other hand, are so closely associated with particular spaces that they almost seem to be a trait of these spaces. Ideas of desired and detested naturalness are embedded in all these spatial ideas and practices. But these historically evolved ideas obstruct our view of other ecologies that surround us.

BLACK HOLE SUN

> At the gates of utopia, it is written: Truth.
> Animals are not allowed.
> —Oxana Timofeeva

We've become so used to being called consumers that we've started to see ourselves mainly in that role. Hence even the desire for political change is framed within a model of consumption. The victory of market-based consciousness could not be more complete. The practical critique of the so-called excesses of capitalism is expressed by purchasing capitalist products.

In psychology there is an expression for a comparable phenomenon, the Stockholm Syndrome. Under certain circumstances, victims of hostage taking show increasing sympathy for their captors—sometimes to the point of total identification with the hostage takers. Faced with having to admit to yourself that you're completely subject to an external power, it can look more attractive to feel that you're part of that power. In the neoliberal ideology of correct consumption, we all become Swedish Dr. Strangeloves, having learned long ago to love the bomb. This bomb is the commodity form. And it has already exploded.

This has created a black hole that is consuming our imagination. In the centre of this black hole there is—a supermarket. "Supermarket" here doesn't mean just the physical place, but the almost all-encompassing compulsion to buy or sell something. In the supermarket, even the idea of justice, which has long been set against the economy, takes on commodity form. After hundreds of thousands of years as a species and thousands of years as a class society, it has only taken a few decades for us to make the supermarket (and its shaggy brother—the organic food store) into the outer limit of the human imagination. Since it seems unthinkable to resist the gravitational pull of the market, we let ourselves fall all the way into it.

When the verdict is a life sentence because we can't even imagine a society beyond capitalism, we start to love the prison bars and have tender feelings for the locked cell door. Strange thoughts arise—Maybe imprisonment is actually liberation? Maybe we can consume our way to a better society? Domination approaches absolute power when every possible way to overcome it can only be imagined in the categories and vocabulary of domination.

OUT OF OUR CLASS

Once the anatomists of neoliberalism have succeeded in declaring the individual wallet to be the main political muscle, suddenly the welfare recipient is just as responsible for the misery of the world as the filthy rich real-estate developer who evicts them. At this point, morality resembles the tax office:

mass taxes are instruments of redistribution. This is also true of the conscience. A flat tax rate that ostensibly puts an equal burden on all income bleeds lower incomes relatively more. This is immediately evident: if you have an income that just barely covers the cost of living, then a tax rate that takes, for example, a fifth of gross income could be a life-threatening situation. On the other hand, if you have a million at your disposal, you can still live high off the hog from what's left over. Although less consciously, the same is true for morality as for taxes: treating what is unequal equally promotes inequality. Making consumers responsible for the conditions of production is a moral tax giveaway for the people who get rich from the production conditions and, on the basis of this wealth, can afford to run away from the repercussions of these processes.

The seeming democratization of responsibility also has the repressive function of counterinsurgency. If the human multitude can be talked into believing that they are responsible for not having a job (or for having a bad one), for animals getting tossed into meat grinders, for rampant global inequality, and for the destruction of the environment, then they will no longer direct their rage at those who occupy the top spots in the economy, politics, or ideology, but aim it at their own kind.

But the logic of correct consumption, whether of fair-trade bananas or organic products, is even more cynical. After all, whoever has more financial means available can buy more high-priced fair-trade consumer products. For the delicate-minded bourgeois this adds another criterion by which to select those luxury comestibles—sustainable fairness. Within the logic of correct consumption, the economically better off are morally superior to the wretched of the earth: whoever has more money can afford not only a bigger home and better quality food, no, they are also potentially better people, because it is vastly easier for them to acquire more fair-trade products.[1] And to top it all off, the exploited and marginalized are now complicit in the exploitation and marginalization of everyone else.

PURITY IS THE VITRIOL OF THE SOUL

In 2015 a short article by Fabian Federl was one of the most widely read articles in the Berlin *Tagesspiegel*.[2] The article consists mainly of a precise description of its vegan subject arranging a line of coke, along with a list of all the human victims and poisonous substances that are bound up with the production of cocaine. Besides that, the article associates cocaine with the upper class. The moral of the story is found in the last sentence: "I find it unbearably dishonest for someone to run around acting morally superior while the blood of murdered Mexicans is stuck to his mucous membranes." As the author tells us, this article is the answer he would like to have given to the vegan snorting coke when she told him the reasons for her veganism. We learn almost nothing about these reasons, but we do get the author's reaction: he nodded to himself and used the search for a beer as an excuse to bow out.

After listing the dead in the drug war, the article continues: "And you, all coked up, are getting upset about how animals are treated?" The portrait that follows, of the "Berliner under thirty from an upscale neighbourhood" includes the contradiction of teaching "German for refugees" and then spending "Friday to Sunday all coked up at Sisyphos" (a Berlin nightclub). Even though the author repeatedly declares that he is indifferent to the use of the drug, the title of the article is clear: "First Stop Doing Coke."

The next year, *Vice Magazine* jumped on the same bandwagon with the article "This Is How Immoral Doing Cocaine Is."[3] Here a young drug dealer in Los Angeles is confronted with the official government figures on deaths in the war on drugs. This guy hadn't even been aware of the violence: "Random people being *offed*, and stuff like that? I don't know anything about it." But one thing is clear to him: "On the consumer side right now, nobody gives a shit. They can be vegan and still blow lines. Human bloodshed is fine for you, but animal bloodshed, no. It's kinda ugly in that sense for sure."

While the author in the *Tagesspiegel* limits himself to accusations of hypocrisy and demands that people stop taking cocaine before they're allowed get politically active, *Vice Magazine* is more conciliatory, adopting a philosophy professor's suggestion that if you have a bad conscience, you should take a cue from corporations that offset their oversized CO_2 footprint by giving to charity. That's what you should do too if your cocaine use has given you a guilty conscience: donate to an organization that supports victims of the drug business.

In 2018 Cressida Dick, the controversial chief of the London police, known colloquially as Scotland Yard, made headlines when she blamed vegans for rising gang violence in London. "This is a problem that goes far beyond policing," said the top policewoman. "There's a whole group of middle class people who will sit round happily thinking about global warming, fair trade, environmental protection and organic food, but think there's no harm in taking a bit of cocaine." But there is: misery runs through the entire supply chain.[4]

Veganism and cocaine seems to be a combination that's robbing some of our fellow citizens of sleep—even if they aren't consuming. Federl's repudiation of flaunting one's moral superiority, which, by the way, we learn nothing more about, is no doubt legitimate. But Federl's argument is not only dripping with a sense of moral superiority, it's also pretty clumsy. That is, his statement, that veganism in people whose unexamined consumption destroys forty-five square feet of rainforest per gram of cocaine is hypocritical, is a so-called knockout argument. The production of just one computer uses up tens of thousands of gallons of water, and just one Google search consumes as much electricity as an energy-saving lightbulb shining for hours. Does that mean we can no longer take someone seriously who owns a computer or once did a Google search?

But what exactly is the vegan's "hypocrisy"? Not wanting to or being able to solve all the world's problems individually and simultaneously? Not caring about people first and only then about animals? Maybe Federl imagines political activists and ordinary vegans as humble ascetics, which doesn't fit in with visions of boundless hedonism.

Federl seems to demand a special form of political purity. But Bruno Latour was right on target when he proclaimed: "Beware of purity; it is the vitriol of the soul."[5] The idea of purity—no matter whether it's physical, spiritual, or political purity—is a bad high. This rotgut won't give you visions, it will make you blind.

UTOPIAN RESISTANCE AT THE PUBLIC POOL

There's lots of talk during moralizing discussions about social and ecological responsibility—but the flipside of this is a rhetorical magnification of the importance of individual decisions. This is a comforting illusion about the strength and agency of each individual. On the other hand, admitting to yourself that you can hardly change anything about the way things are by making consumer decisions is a bitter pill for narcissistic egos accustomed to mistaking themselves for saviours of the world in the mirror of their supposed market power. Theodor W. Adorno's dictum in *Minima Moralia* has not lost any of its truth: "The almost insoluble task is to let neither the power of others, nor our own powerlessness, stupefy us."[6]

There will be no salvation in the ideology of correct consumption—save for those who make more or less good money selling these products, or for those who experience this ideology as a comforting sedative (at least I'm doing "something").

Stupidity, on the other hand, is often part of utopian life. Every summer day at a public outdoor pool in Vienna—the well-maintained Laaerberg Pool, which is frequented by the working and migrant classes—a large group of kids and teens behave stupidly in a politically wonderful way. One of the most popular attractions at this pool is the wave pool, where every hour on the hour artificial waves are generated for ten minutes. As expected, the general delight comes to an end after ten minutes, but the sound of the waves is punctually replaced by a surge of booing, yelling, laughing, and whistling rising from the throats of dozens of children and teenagers. This is how they protest the end of the fun.

This is undoubtedly "stupid," because every realist and pragmatist knows that there must be a reason for limiting the rhythm and duration of the waves. Certainly it is also "stupid" to think that the responsible parties would ever respond to the protests. The political in this case consists in the collective contradiction that at once celebrates swimming together and sun on wet skin and the privilege of being alive at precisely this moment. Sometimes a dog being walked outside the pool fence starts to bark along.

All joy wants eternity, wrote Friedrich Nietzsche.[7] And the utopian begins with the struggle against death, as Theodor W. Adorno and Ernst Bloch put it.[8] The utopian revolt against the pragmatism of *realpolitik* has its origins in the disregard for the only certainty we possess: all human beings (and animals) must die. Whether the children of the laughing revolt know all of this consciously is beside the point: they are animated by the communist esprit.

SOCIAL REVOLUTIONARY THREE-YEAR-OLDS

As a matter of fact, there are also social-revolutionary powers lurking in vegetarianism and veganism (veg*). These do not lie in the restructuring of the economy by means of correct consumption. All the vegetarians and vegans of the world haven't saved a single animal from unnecessary death; capitalist economy doesn't work this way. Not only is overproduction a structural characteristic of market-driven societies, subsidies and secondary markets stabilize possible declines in sales. The vision of an incremental growth of non-meat resembles the old social-democratic myth of linear progress at the election polls until 51 percent of the votes are achieved and socialism can be installed. Never in political history did this model succeed. That doesn't mean that it is entirely impossible, only in reality it is probably far more complex and non-linear than commonly thought. In no way does this mean that veg* is meaningless; on the contrary, its political importance could just be something besides a direct way to achieve a goal.

There is nothing true about vegetarianism and veganism but their exaggerations.

The utopian powers of veg* lie in the disruption of the normal state of things, not in their normalization in the form of veggie-burger chains. To live veg* means to break materially and symbolically with the prevailing conditions. Doing so doesn't require taking a course in political education or being able to write an essay in political theory.

When I was still a teenager, I once accompanied my mother to visit a Turkish friend of hers. She had a three-year-old daughter who had become a vegetarian overnight after finding out where the sujuk sausage on her plate came from. When preschool children stop eating meat, they are breaking with a whole world of the adults: book learning that declares social violence to be a natural part of food chains; social norms that affirm the culture of the slaughterhouse to be a normal condition; religions that make it a divine right to go for someone else's throat. A three-year-old is ready to take on family, school, government, society, science, and God, all at the same time. The utopian-communist moment seen here consists in the break with all social and ideological powers.

The crucial point here is the break. A break is like a pregnancy: it's all or nothing. You can't make a break like that halfway (less meat) or fake it (organic meat)—otherwise it's not a break. The specificity of literally devouring others asks us to rethink the materiality of the symbolic. You can't burn your bridges half down or only pretend to torch them when what is at stake is exploring the utopian continent of solidarity. Veg* forces us to rethink what is utopian.

MAKING THE PRESENT STUTTER

In the great traditions of Western thought, utopias were imagined as distant in time or as isolated space containers. Utopia was either shifted into the past as a lost Garden of Eden or postponed into the future of a final victory over capitalism. Utopias were set on desert islands or other planets, in model worlds or colonies. The utopia of veg*, on the other hand, is an art of the present, a rebellion against normality.

The intelligence of veg* does not lie in realizing that fewer resources will be consumed if we finally stop chopping down forests and planting soybean monocultures in their place, only to shovel vast amounts of this food into animals that we then kill in order to get a fairly puny amount of meat. That is nothing but the planetary accountant's logic of ecocapitalism, which urges us to monitor ourselves more excessively than social media, Internet cookies, or the National Security Agency ever could. With this metaphor of the earth as a precarious spaceship, the eco-accountants of the world only want to make us constantly evaluate everything we do in terms of resource saving and sustainable efficiency, so that we either save or buy something somewhere. Ideally both.

Nor does the power of veg* lie in the promise that we will be much healthier and live longer—because this is biopolitics in its purest form: Michel Foucault used this term for those modern techniques of power that not only squeeze the subservient with physical force and religious intimidation, but also employ a bunch of scientific techniques to get them to be more productive while dominating them more and more. Today it is talk of lean government and fit bodies that is promising a thousand-year empire of health for both nations and individuals.

The beauty of veg* also doesn't lie in being able to inhabit a higher moral plane, from which we can smile down on the less enlightened. Good and evil as moral categories are leftovers from feudalism that are still just good enough, as undead zombies, for keeping professional ethics boards alive.

The militancy of veg* consists not in the clever reform or modern management of circumstances, but in the excessive, practical, and symbolic break with their logics.

Veg*, so understood, allows new organs of solidarity to grow. A sentence by Franz Kafka points in this direction. His friend Max Brod told about the occasion of a visit to the Berlin Aquarium:

> Then he spoke to the fishes in the illuminated boxes. "Now that I can look at you in peace, I won't eat you anymore." It was at the time when he had become a strict vegetarian. If one hasn't heard such pronouncements from Kafka himself, one can hardly conceive how simply and easily, without all affectation, without the slightest pathos (which was almost completely foreign to him) he said such things.[9]

With reference to this sentence (which is seldom missing from any collection of quotations on the theme "Clever vegetarians say clever things about vegetarianism"), Kafka's vegetarianism has variously been associated with artistic asceticism and the rejection of his paternal line (his grandfather was a kosher butcher), with shame and forgetting, or with early Christianity.[10] But let's stay with the aspect of the tranquil gaze, which plays a minor role in the various interpretations.

The gaze harbours a precarious power: when the mythical hero Oedipus committed the worst imaginable sacrilege and slept with his mother, he didn't cry out that he wanted to castrate himself, but rather swore never to look at a woman again. In Sophocles's version of the myth, Oedipus gouges out his eyes. And it is said of Afghan queens that heralds announced their arrival to the people with the order "Go blind!" This was a command to lower their eyes and at the same time an admission that even the lowest underprivileged landless man had the power of a disrespectful gaze.

Kafka's sentence can be understood as a reminder that it makes a difference how we observe the world around us: with the hungry eyes of absorption and incorporation, or as a—sometimes repugnant, disturbing, uncanny, dangerous—source of fascination?

THE DECOLONIZATION OF THE SENSES

The short story *The Persistence of Vision* (1978)[11] by science fiction author John Herbert Varley gives us an idea of what it might mean to decolonize not only the mind, but the senses as well. The science officer of the Starship *Enterprise* might respond to this by saying: fascinating.

At the centre of the short story is a utopian commune that was founded by a group of deaf and blind people in a postapocalyptic setting of ecological destruction so they could live an autarkic life without the limitations of the sighted and hearing world.

The story is told from the perspective of a nameless visitor through whose eyes we get to know the mores and customs of this community. At first glance, for example, communication in this place called Keller (as in Helen Keller) looks to a sighted visitor like an orgy: the naked residents incessantly communicate using every part of their bodies and making themselves understood by means of nuances and intimacies of expression beyond the capacity of the visitor. Moreover, the commune seems to be free of racism, sexism, capitalism, and violence. After a lengthy, instructive stay the narrator finally leaves the utopian community of Keller—not because he couldn't integrate himself, but because it becomes clear to him how much communication and communion must remain denied to him. The curious happy ending of this story consists in his happy return to Keller after he too has lost his abilities to see and hear.

In Varley's Keller, though the protagonist is initially unsettled by the unaccustomed communicative choreographies of the naked commune residents, he does immediately feel a certain superiority as well: his position of the all-seeing, unmarked gaze assigns to the deaf and blind people the position of being marked and disadvantaged. In contrast with them, he has the power of seeing without being seen—and at the same time, willingly or unwillingly, he starts to experience a feeling of voyeurism. In the course of the story, however, this feeling turns into its opposite, because the deaf and blind residents of Keller communicate not via the usual "mouthtalk," but only via "handtalk," not only spelling out concepts using finger gestures in the palms of their interlocutor's hands, but also using more refined and more complex nonverbal means of communication like "shorthand," "bodytalk," and "touch." It becomes clear to the protagonist that the residents "see" differently, but not less or worse. They make themselves understood with their bodies and their sense of touch and, as Varley suggests, they have also cultivated other faculties. What looks to the sighted like an incessant orgy of the deaf and blind is actually a form of continuous pansexuality, not genitally focused, of everyone with everyone. The narrator too concludes that in Keller, polymorphous sexuality and communication were indistinguishable: ". . . with a hundred naked bodies sliding, rubbing, kissing, caressing, all at the same time, what was the point in making a distinction? There was no distinction."[12]

Varley's short story may very likely fall short of today's standards. For example it is not clear if he ever asked a blind person to describe their actual experience or if the whole story is an imaginative and well-intentioned, yet excessively romanticizing endeavour (including typical post-1968 ideas of sexual liberation). At the same time the little story proved influential for activists, artists, and scholars, as a non-innocent inspiration and lasting challenge for understanding what it is like to be an other (human or non-human, real or imaginary). Literature is one of many ways to try to connect with others and their life worlds.

There is a power of fictional voices acknowledging that listening closely for new voices in the realm of the imagination can enable us to hear more clearly the most compelling and urgent voices in reality. Eva Hayward carries the non-deficit-oriented argument of Varley's story across species boundaries and takes cnidarians, whose eyes, sex organs, and fingers merge into one another, as the starting point of her re-envisioning of the concepts and categories of knowledge and meaning production.[13] In her search for alternatives to the all-knowing eye of the Enlightenment, Hayward asks what the more-than-visual "images" constituted in the "head" of cnidarians may be like.

SOLIDARITY IS THE TENDERNESS OF THE SPECIES

Grappling with these partial perspectives can be politically fascinating. For the philosophizing poet Timothy Morton, precisely "our capacity for fascination is what fuels solidarity": "Fascination is the aesthetic gravitational attraction of entities toward one another, the dynamics of solidarity, within a force-field-like matrix of sensitivities."[14]

Solidary humanity for Morton does not mean the ascetic renunciation of pleasure, but being able to enjoy another's pleasure. The communism that Morton envisions can only be "contingent, fragile and playful":[15]

> You become fascinated by enhancing and expanding non-human pleasure modes. In this way, vegetarianism (for example) is not about opposing cruelty or minimizing suffering or enhancing one's health by returning to a more natural way of eating, but about a pleasure mode designed to maintain or enhance the pleasure modes of pigs or cows or sheep and so on.[16]

For Morton, ecological consciousness means knowing that someone will always be left out in the rain. Helping an animal can mean starving another animal that would have liked to feed on it. "This necessary exclusion is the locus of violence, such that solidarity is always in the structural position of wishing it could encompass more, encompass everything."[17]

What can this mean for a political relationship with animals? The concept of solidarity goes back to Roman law, where the "solidarity principle" meant that every participant in a solidary association is individually and wholly responsible for every other one. In other words: solidarity is indivisible and it does not come without a cost. Moreover, solidarity not only means always risking your own skin, but also knows no boundaries. It is excessive.

THE GREAT SHOW OF SYMPATHY

For a long time, a program called *Licht ins Dunkel* (Light into the Darkness) was the most popular charity show on Austrian public television. At Christmastime, celebrities would ask business luminaries and private citizens for donations to projects for the disabled. TV ads for the charity gala featured the voice of a young person anxiously calling into the darkness: "Is anybody there?"

This is how many like to imagine people who are handicapped by the social reality: as pitiful victims, languishing in the darkness—until the sovereign possessors of mental and physical powers finally rescue them by writing a cheque. What may trigger comforting emotions in private donors and represent for corporations a favourable opportunity to polish their image has become the object of insistent criticism from disability rights organizations and activists. What's happening here is the cementing of a deficit-oriented image of human beings who do not conform physically or mentally to the norm. While these TV programs reduce socially disabled people to being seen first as needy and later as overjoyed recipients of handouts and solicitude, more and more initiatives are demanding support for their struggle, not mere charity.

Today, militant associations of people with non-standard bodies who revolt against the social production of neediness may seem utopian to some, but even in the 1970s, with initiatives like the German "Cripple Movement," they were already reality.[18]

Every progressive movement must proceed from the activity of the affected people themselves. They don't have to remain alone—otherwise the word "solidarity" would have no meaning. But erasing the self-activity of those affected means nothing less than reverting to patronizing paternalism or technocratic fantasies of government advocacy.

Recently, campaigns that wish to appear politically progressive have striven to avoid situating people handicapped by society in victim choreographies, staging them rather as heroes of everyday life. However, this new heroization is only the other side of the same coin determined by outsiders. This bipolar division recalls comparable doublings: whether women are portrayed as holy mothers or promiscuous whores; or Muslim people appear only as enslaved women or enraged men; or Indigenous societies are dismissed as less than human or idealized as "noble savages"—all of this reveals more about the structures of desire of those projecting the images than about the reality of those being portrayed.

A CHICKEN NAMED JESUS

Initiatives in animal politics often draw on religious tropes in order to generate concern for their causes. Who hasn't seen it? Animal welfare activists or animal rights advocates stand in public spaces, holding up posters showing maltreated and martyred animals. "They died for you!" is a common slogan, addressing either people who wear furs or people who eat meat. In collages reminiscent of splatter films, the "battery hen" is turned into some kind of tragic Christ figure: suffered in vain.

At the same time, the homey dining room table is transformed into a Middle Eastern Golgotha, where the crucifixion of this poor creature is carried out several times a day. Instead of promises of salvation, there are recriminations and the hope for a guilty conscience. After all, today's consumers don't have the excuse the Roman legionnaires had back then: they do know what they do—at least once they've stopped at the info table.

Even if the participants belong to different social milieus, there are ideological continuities in the "sin and sacrifice" rhetoric around animals that can be traced back to the context of the beginnings of the first animal welfare groups. These groups arose together with bourgeois child-protection and workers' protection organizations—initiated by well-intentioned and well-situated forces who wanted to take care of the people "down there" from "up here." This kind of paternalistic moralism has as much to do with progressive politics as Ronald McDonald has to do with Rosa Luxemburg.

One of the many problems associated with this strategic approach is that the thinking and presentation repeat exactly what its opponents get accused of—the violent subjugation of animals. But the violence here is epistemic violence, that is, the violence that lies in ideas and concepts. While industry, biological science, and agriculture immobilize animals using physical devices, animal victimology does the same thing by declaring animals to be eternal victims and making their resistance imperceptible.

Astoundingly, workers' organizations and trade unions usually don't take a position on the animal question that is qualitatively different from those of the conservatives and reactionaries. In seminars and on magazine pages, everything is open for debate: gender relations and child rearing, housing construction and forms of interment. But for many on the left, animals seem to represent the last space that is devoid of politics. This space should be politicized and radicalized, analyzed and recontextualized—in terms of both the historical-affective blocs that we call animals and their long discursive shadows.

GORILLA GUERRILLAS IN THE MIST

Confronting the Fordist factory system, Antonio Gramsci pointed to the man who scientifically rationalized the work process, Frederick Winslow Taylor, stressing that the assembly line turned human beings into "trained gorillas." In parts of the West, today's creative imperative[19] is perhaps calling for a post-Fordist subject that is more of an "experimental city monkey," who animates unused urban spaces with creative-industrial interim-use projects, playfully drives innovation, and gets high on drugs on the weekend so they can practise their social skills for Monday. It should be expected that communism, as an unredeemed promise of humanity, will let the apes out of the zoos—physically and metaphorically.

What Marx wrote about the relationship between English and Irish workers also holds for the relationship between humans and animals: there can be no freedom as long as there is still unfreedom. We may not yet be able to fully picture what this might mean, but there is no reason we should not begin to imagine it. To use words and images, emotions and deeds to make reality stutter, as in the seemingly utopian vision of—gorilla guerrillas in the mist.

NOTES

INTRODUCTION

1. Cf. Marilyn Strathern, *Partial Connections* (Lanham, MD: AltaMira Press, 2004).
2. Karl Marx, *Letters from the Deutsch-Französische Jahrbücher, Collected Works* (London: Lawrence and Wishart, 2004) (MECW), vol. 3: Marx and Engels 1833–1844, 145.
3. Anett Laue, *Das sozialistische Tier: Auswirkungen der SED-Politik auf gesellschaftliche Mensch-Tier-Verhältnisse in der DDR (1949–1989)* (Köln: Böhlau Verlag, 2017).
4. Karl Marx and Friedrich Engels, *Manifesto of the Communist Party*, MECW, vol. 6: Marx and Engels 1845–1848, 513.
5. Laue, *Das sozialistische Tier*, 294ff.
6. Laue, *Das sozialistische Tier*, 311.
7. Karl Marx and Friedrich Engels, "G. Fr. Daumer, 'Die Religion des neuen Weltalters. Versuch einer combinatorisch-aphoristischen Grundlegung', 2 Bde., Hamburg 1850" [Reviews from the *Neue Rheinische Zeitung*, "Politisch-Ökonomische Revue" No. 2, February 1850], MECW, vol. 7, 241–46, 242.
8. Will Potter, *Green Is the New Red: An Insider's Account of*

a Social Movement under Siege (San Francisco: City Lights Books, 2011).

9. MECW, vol. 35: Marx, 187–208, 188. (The original sentence is literally: ". . . that he makes the cells in his head, before he makes them in wax."—Tr.)
10. Cf. Timothy Mitchell, *Rule of Experts: Egypt, Techno-Politics, and Modernity* (University of California Press, Berkeley, 2002), 45.
11. Maria Kaika, "Dams as Symbols of Modernization: The Urbanization of Nature between Geographical Imagination and Materiality," *Annals of the Association of American Geographers* 96,2 (2006), 276–301.
12. David Harvey, *A Companion to Marx's Capital* (New York: Verso, 2010), 112.
13. Donna Haraway, *When Species Meet* (Minneapolis/London: University of Minnesota Press, 2008), 46, 67, 73.
14. John Berger, "Why Look at Animals?" in *About Looking* (New York: Bloomsbury, 1980), 1–26. Cf. Jonathan Burt, "John Berger's 'Why Look at Animals?': A Close Reading," *Worldviews: Global Religions, Culture, and Ecology* 9,2 (2005), 203–218.
15. For some exceptions that confirm the rule, see Jason Hribal, *Fear of the Animal Planet: The Hidden History of Animal Resistance* (Oakland: AK Press, 2011); Jonathan L. Clark, "Labourers or Lab Tools? Rethinking the Role of Lab Animals in Clinical Trials," in *The Rise of Critical Animal Studies: From the Margins to the Centre* ed. Nik Taylor and Richard Twine (London: Routledge, 2014), 139–66; Ted Benton, *Natural Relations: Ecology, Animal Rights & Social*

Justice (London/New York: Verso, 1993); Lawrence Wilde, "'The Creatures, Too, Must Become Free': Marx and the Animal/Human Distinction," *Capital & Class* 72 (2000), 37–53; Agnieszka Kowalczyk, "Mapping Non-human Resistance in the Age of Biocapital," in *The Rise of Critical Animal Studies*, 183–200.

16. Marx and Engels, MECW, vol. 50, 466.
17. Marx and Engels, MECW, vol. 50, 466.

PIGEON POLITICS

1. Woody Allen's Film *Stardust Memories* (1980), to which this political metaphor is often erroneously attributed, contains the following dialogue between Sandy (Allen) and Dorrie, when a pigeon flies into her apartment.
   Dorrie: "Hey, that's so pretty. A pigeon!"
   Sandy: "Geez, no. It's not pretty at all. They're, they're, they're rats with wings."
   Dorrie: "They're wonderful. No! It's probably a good omen. It'll bring us good luck."
   Sandy: "No, no. Get it out of here. It's probably one of those killer pigeons."
2. For the sake of readability, especially in the historical passages, references have been dispensed with in the text here. The information given here can be located in the following works and texts: Horst Marks, *Unsere Haustauben* (Wittenberg: Ziemsen, 1971); Andrea Dee, *Eine vergessene Leidenschaft: Von Tauben und Menschen* (Wien: Ueberreuter, 1994); Richard Johnston and Marián Janiga,

Feral Pigeons (New York: Oxford University Press, 1995); Daniel Haag-Wackernagel, *Die Taube: Vom heiligen Vogel der Liebesgöttin zur Strassentaube* (Basel: Verlag Schwabe & Co, 1998); David Glover and Marie Beaumont, *Racing Pigeons* (Marlborough: Crowood, 1999); Annette Rösener, *Die Stadttaubenproblematik: Ursachen, Entwicklungen, Lösungen; eine Literatur-Übersicht* (Aachen: Shaker, 1999); Andrew Blechman, *Pigeons* (New York: Grove Press, 2006); Simon J. Bronner, "Contesting Tradition: The Deep Play and Protest of Pigeon Shoots," *Journal of American Folklore* 118 (2005), 409–452; Eva Rose, Peter Nagel, and Daniel Haag-Wackernagel, "Spatio-temporal Use of the Urban Habitat by Feral Pigeons (*Columba livia*)," *Behavioral Ecology and Sociobiology* 60,2 (2006), 242–54; Günther Vater, "Bestandsverminderung bei verwilderten Haustauben. Teil 1: Bilanz mitteleuropäischer Stadtverwaltungen," *Bundesgesundheitsblatt–Gesundheitsforschung–Gesundheitsschutz* 42,12 (1999), 911–21; Courtney Humphries, *Superdove: How the Pigeon Took Manhattan—and the World* (New York: Collins, 2008).

3. Hans-Georg Soeffner, "Der fliegende Maulwurf (Der taubenzüchtende Bergmann im Ruhrgebiet)—totemistische Verzauberung und technologische Entzauberung der Sehnsucht" in *Paradoxien, Dissonanzen, Zusammenbrüche*, ed. Hans Ulrich Gumbrecht and Karl Ludwig Pfeiffer (Frankfurt am Main: Suhrkamp, 1990), 431–53, 439.

4. For an amusing literary portrayal of the battle against pigeons—from the point of view of the pigeons—see

Patrick Neates, *The London Pigeon Wars* (London: Penguin, 2004).
5. Colin Jerolmack, "How Pigeons Became Rats: The Cultural-Spatial Logic of Problem Animals," *Social Problems* 55,2 (2008), 72–94, 72.
6. Cf. Mary Douglas, *Purity and Danger: An Analysis of Concepts of Pollution and Taboo* (London: Routledge, 1966).
7. Quoting from Bernhard Kathan, "Human, unauffällig: Gehn mer Tauben vergiften im Park," *Die Gazette*, July 12, 2001.
8. Kathan, "Human, unauffällig."
9. Cf. Jacques Derrida, *The Beast and the Sovereign: The Seminars of Jacques Derrida*, vol. I, trans. Geoffrey Bennington (Chicago: University of Chicago Press, 2009), 23.
10. Hans-Hermann Kotte, "Tauben-Population geht zurück," *Frankfurter Rundschau*, July 12, 2012.
11. Cf. Michel Foucault, "What Is Critique?" in *The Politics of Truth*, ed. Sylvère Lotringer and Lysa Hochroth (New York: Semiotext(e), 1997), transcript by Monique Emery, revised by Suzanne Delorme, et al., translated into English by Lysa Hochroth (originally French 1978), 28.
12. But they are by no means alone: beasts of burden like donkeys and mules for example have turned up in high modernist architectural discourses and ethnological thought about cities when questions of authority and obstinacy were addressed. See Catherine Ingraham, *Architecture and The Burdens of Linearity* (New Haven: Yale University Press, 1998).
13. In Great Britain the phenomenon of "granarchists" is well known. They often form the most militant part of animal

rights demonstrations and with their visible presence at the forefront of illegal protests sometimes inhibit even hardened riot cops from striking blows.

SWINISH MULTITUDES

1. Thomas Macho, *Schweine: Ein Porträt*, Naturkunden 17, ed. Judith Schalansky (Berlin: Matthes & Seitz, 2015), 9f.
2. Paul A. Gilje, *The Road to Mobocracy: Popular Disorder in New York City, 1763–1834* (Chapel Hill: University of North Carolina Press, 1987), 228.
3. Howard B. Rock, "A Delicate Balance: The Mechanics and the City," *New York Historical Quarterly* 63 (April 1979), 93–114.
4. Charles Rosenberg, *The Cholera Years: The United States in 1832, 1949 and 1966* (Chicago: University of Chicago Press, 1962), 17, cited in Hendrik Hartok, "Pigs and Positivism," *University of Wisconsin Law Review* 4 (1985), 899–935, 921.
5. Catherine McNeur, "The 'Swinish Multitude': Controversies over Hogs in Antebellum New York City," *Journal of Urban History* 37,5 (2011), 639–60, 640.
6. Hartok, "Pigs and Positivism," 905f.
7. Catherine McNeur, *Taming Manhattan: Environmental Battles in the Antebellum City* (Cambridge, MA: Harvard University Press, 2014), 23–44.
8. McNeur, *Taming Manhattan*, 38. McNeur conjectures that the restriction in the same year of the civil rights of a large group of insurgents, the African-Americans, sharply limited the possibility of dealing differently with the pig hunt.

9. Gilje, *Road to Mobocracy*, 228f.
10. Gilje, *Road to Mobocracy*, 230.
11. McNeur, *Taming Manhattan*, 40.
12. Nádia Farage, "No Collar, No Master: Workers and Animals in the Modernization of Rio de Janeiro, 1903–4," in *Transcultural Modernisms*, ed. Fahim Amir, Eva Egermann, Moira Hille, Jakob Krameritsch, Christian Kravagna, Christina Linortner, Marion von Osten, and Peter Spillmann (Berlin: Sternberg Press, 2013), 110–20, 111.
13. McNeur, *Taming Manhattan*, 24.
14. The complete title is *Reflections on the Revolution in France, and on the Proceedings in Certain Societies in London Relative to That Event. In a Letter Intended to Have Been Sent to a Gentleman in Paris.*
15. "Give not that which is holy unto the dogs, neither cast ye your pearls before swine, lest they trample them under their feet, and turn again and rend you" (Matthew 7:6, King James Version).
16. Edmund Burke, *Reflections on the Revolution in France, 1790* (London, 1820), vol. 1, 109f.
17. Carl Fisher, "Politics and Porcine Representation: Multitudinous Swine in the British Eighteenth Century," *Lit: Literature Interpretation Theory* 10,4 (1999), 303–326, 306.
18. Fisher, "Politics and Porcine Representation," 303.
19. Mark Neocleous, *The Monstrous and the Dead: Burke, Marx, Fascism* (Cardiff: University of Wales Press, 2005), 5f.
20. Cf. Stephen Eisenman, "The Real 'Swinish Multitude,'" *Critical Inquiry* 42,2 (2016), 339–73.
21. Eisenman, "The Real 'Swinish Multitude,'" 349.

22. Eisenman, "The Real 'Swinish Multitude,'" 343.
23. Eisenman, "The Real 'Swinish Multitude,'" 344.
24. Eisenman, "The Real 'Swinish Multitude,'" 343, citing *Public Advertiser*, May 10, 1790.
25. Eisenman, "The Real 'Swinish Multitude,'" 351, citing John Middleton, *View of the Agriculture of Middlesex: With Observations on the Means of Its Improvement* (London, 1798).
26. Eisenman, "The Real 'Swinish Multitude,'" 350.
27. Eisenman, "The Real 'Swinish Multitude,'" 352.
28. Eisenman, "The Real 'Swinish Multitude,'" 347.
29. Marx and Engels, *Manifesto of the Communist Party*, 492.
30. Eisenman, "The Real 'Swinish Multitude,'" 348.
31. Friedrich Engels, *The Condition of the Working Class in England*, MECW, vol. 4, 295–583, 354.
32. Engels, *Condition of the Working Class*, 286, 356.
33. Mark Neocleous, *The Universal Adversary: Security, Capital and "the Enemies of All Mankind"* (Abingdon/Oxon/New York: Routledge, 2016), 31.
34. Neocleous, *The Universal Adversary*, 26f.
35. Fisher, "Politics and Porcine Representation," 319.
36. Olivia Smith, *The Politics of Language, 1791–1916* (Oxford: Clarendon, 1984), 81.
37. Fisher, "Politics and Porcine Representation," 320.
38. See for example Darren Howard, "Necessary Fictions: The 'Swinish Multitude' and the Rights of Man," *Studies in Romanticism* 47,2 (Summer 2008), 161–78.
39. Eisenman: "The Real 'Swinish Multitude,'" 361.
40. Neocleous, *The Monstrous and the Dead*, 34.

41. Macho, *Schweine*, 23.
42. Antonio Negri and Michael Hardt, *Empire* (Cambridge, MA: Harvard University Press, 2000); *Multitude: War and Democracy in the Age of Empire* (New York: Penguin, 2004). These new approaches speak of post-workerism, since post-structuralist theories were increasingly accepted following the smashing of workerist organizations in Italy and the exile in France of many workerists. Post-workerist theorizing attributes hegemonic weight to immaterial production and emphasizes intellectual and linguistic aspects of contemporary productivity. See Pascal Jurt, "Menschliche Bienen. Interview mit Yann Moulier Boutang zur Entstehung und möglichen Überwindung des 'kognitiven Kapitalismus'" [Human Bees: Interview with Yann Moulier Boutang on the Arising and Possible Overcoming of "Cognitive Capitalism"], *springerin. Magazin zur Kritik und Theorie der Kultur der Gegenwart* 4 (2014).
43. Cf. Paolo Virno, *A Grammar of the Multitude for an Analysis of Contemporary Forms of Life*, trans. Isabella Bertoletti, James Cascaito, and Andrea Casson (Los Angeles: Semiotexte, 2004), 26.
44. See also Matthew Chrulew, "Animals in Biopolitical Theory: Between Agamben and Negri," *New Formations* 76 (2012), 53–67, 59–63.
45. Alain Ehrenberg, *The Weariness of the Self: Diagnosing the History of Depression in the Contemporary Age* (Montreal and Kingston: McGill-Queen's University Press, 2010).
46. Melanie Joy, *Why We Love Dogs, Eat Pigs, and Wear Cows: An*

Introduction to Carnism (Newburyport, MA: Conari Press, 2009), 43.

47. Cf. Joel Novek, "Pigs and People: Sociological Perspectives on the Discipline of Nonhuman Animals in Intensive Confinement," *Society & Animals* 13,3 (2005), 221–44, 229.
48. Alex Blanchette, "Herding Species: Biosecurity, Posthuman Labor, and the American Industrial Pig," *Cultural Anthropology* 30,4 (2015), 640–69. In the following, Blanchette's theses and results are presented; for the sake of readability, detailed description and citations have been foregone.
49. The Society for Cultural Anthropology (SCA) Biennial Meeting, "The Ends of Work," Detroit, May 2014.
50. Thomas Macho, *Das Leben nehmen: Suizid in der Moderne* (Berlin: Suhrkamp, 2017), 28.
51. Macho, *Das Leben nehmen*, 30. For an in-depth analysis of the notion of war as an adequate description of human-animal relations, see Dinesh Wadiwel, *The War against Animals* (Leiden: Brill Rodopi, 2015).

THE BIRTH OF THE FACTORY

1. Max Horkheimer, "The Skyscraper," in *Dawn & Decline: Notes, 1926–1931 and 1950–1969*, trans. Michael Shaw (New York: Seabury Press, 1978), 66ff.
2. Thus Lewis Mumford's popular book *Sticks and Stones* (1924), a portrayal of American architecture from a social-critical point of view, published by Bruno Cassirer in German translation under the title *Vom Blockhaus zum*

Wolkenkratzer (From Log Cabin to Skyscraper). Bruno Fierl pithily summarizes the connection between publishing politics and the German emotional landscape: "With that he hit exactly upon the image Germans had of America: yesterday a log cabin, today a skyscraper!" (Bruno Fierl, "Nachwort," in Lewis Mumford, *Vom Blockhaus zum Wolkenkratzer: Eine Studie über amerikanische Architektur und Zivilisation*, tr. M. Mauthner (Berlin: Cassirer, 1997; reprint of 1925 edition), 293–304, 301.) It didn't matter that log cabins were hardly mentioned in the book. For German self-confidence, American skyscrapers remained both a humiliation and a challenge.

3. Theodor W. Adorno, *Negative Dialectics*, tr. E.B. Ashton (New York: Seabury Press, 1973), 366.
4. Max Horkheimer, *Gesammelte Schriften*, vol. 7 (Frankfurt a. M.: Suhrkamp, 1985 [1959]), 104.
5. Horkheimer, *Gesammelte Schriften*, vol. 7, 40. With so much cultural achievement internalized and reaching into the body, the recoil is not long in coming: in the phenomenon of *pathic projection*, one's own pleasure-frustration, which builds up through the drilling in of achievement-oriented norms, is violently discharged at the sight of those who do not seem to subordinate their sensitivities to purposeful goals—and is directed with particular intensity against those who exist right before you as "lazy pigs," so to speak.
6. Theodor W. Adorno, *Negative Dialektik* (Frankfurt a. M.: Suhrkamp, 1996 [1966]), 357. (The Ashton translation uses "mansion" in place of "palace."—Tr.)

7. Hannah Higgins, *The Grid Book* (Cambridge MA: MIT Press, 2009), 1.
8. See Richard F. Bales, *The Great Chicago Fire and the Myth of Mrs. O'Leary's Cow* (Jefferson: McFarland, 2002).
9. Sigfried Giedion, *Mechanization Takes Command: A Contribution to Anonymous History* (New York: Oxford University Press, 1948).
10. Sigfried Giedion, *Die Herrschaft der Mechanisierung. Ein Beitrag zur anonymen Geschichte* (Frankfurt a. M.: Europäische Verlagsanstalt, 1982), 782.
11. Hans Magnus Enzensberger, "Über S. Giedions 'Die Herrschaft der Mechanisierung,'" *Der Spiegel*, Feb. 7, 1983, 196–201, 199.
12. Douglas Tallack, "Sigfried Giedion: Modernism and American Material Culture," *Journal of American Studies* 28,2 (1994), 149–67, 157.
13. The significance of this chapter for the project *Mechanization Takes Command* as a whole is underlined by designs for the book's dust jacket. While Giedion himself took charge of the selection and positioning of the many images in *Mechanization Takes Command*, and was able to win Herbert Bayer for its realization, he worked together on the jacket cover design with Stamo Papadaki, who, like Giedion, was active in the CIAM. Three of the drafts distilled the encounter of organic bodies and mechanization in montages in which a "bright red imbued close up of meat was overlaid with technical drawings from the 19th century" (Werner Oechslin and Gregor Harbusch, *Sigfried Giedion und die Fotografie. Bildinszenierungen der*

Moderne (Zürich: Institut für Geschichte und Theorie der Architektur, 2010), 268.)

14. For an overview of the development of the American slaughterhouse industry before and after Cincinnati/Chicago, see Amy J. Fitzgerald, "A Social History of the Slaughterhouse: From Inception to Contemporary Implications," *Human Ecology Review* 17,1 (2010), 58–69.
15. Cf. Marco D'Eramo, *"The Pig and the Skyscraper": Chicago; A History of the Future* (New York: Verso, 2003).
16. Cf. Dominic A. Pacyga, *Slaughterhouse: Chicago's Union Stock Yards and the World It Made* (Chicago: Chicago University Press, 2015), 30–61.
17. Giedion, *Mechanization Takes Command*, 214.
18. Giedion, *Mechanization Takes Command*, 224.
19. William Cronon, *Nature's Metropolis: Chicago and the Great West* (New York: W.W. Norton, 1991), 224.
20. Michael Malay, "Modes of Production, Modes of Seeing: Creaturely Suffering in Upton Sinclair's *The Jungle*," in *American Beasts: Perspectives on Animals, Animality and U.S. Culture, 1776–1920*, ed. Dominik Ohrem (Berlin: Neofelis, 2017), 123–49, 146.
21. Cronon, *Nature's Metropolis*, 251.
22. Cf. Nicole Shukin, *Animal Capital: Rendering Life in Biopolitical Times* (Minneapolis, MN: University of Minnesota Press, 2009), 68.
23. Giedion, *Mechanization Takes Command*, 216.
24. Giedion, *Mechanization Takes Command*, 232.
25. Giedion, *Mechanization Takes Command*, 232.
26. Sigfried Giedion, *Bauen in Frankreich, Bauen in Eisen,*

Bauen in Eisenbeton (Leipzig: Klinkhardt & Biermann, 1928; reprint: Berlin: Gebr. Mann, 2000).

27. Giedion, *Mechanization Takes Command*, 232.
28. Giedion, *Mechanization Takes Command*, 233.
29. Giedion, *Mechanization Takes Command*, 95.
30. Pacyga, *Slaughterhouse*, 66f. On the further development of the American slaughterhouse industry, see Dawn Coppin, "Foucauldian Hog Futures," *Sociological Quarterly* 44,4 (2003), 597–616; Novek, "Pigs and People"; Stephen Thierman, "Apparatuses of Animality: Foucault Goes to a Slaughterhouse," *Foucault Studies* 9 (2010), 89–110.
31. Markus Kurth, "Ausbruch aus dem Schlachthof. Momente der Irritation in der industriellen Tierproduktion durch tierliche Agency," in *Das Handeln der Tiere. Tierliche Agency im Fokus der Human-Animal Studies*, ed. Sven Wirth, Anett Laue, Markus Kurth, Katharina Dornenzweig, Leonie Bossert, Karsten Balgar (Bielefeld: Transcript, 2016), 179–209, 186.
32. Giedion, *Mechanization Takes Command*, 93–94.
33. Giedion, *Mechanization Takes Command*, 236–38.
34. Cf. Mario Tronti, *Workers and Capital* (London/New York: Verso, 2019); Steve Wright, *Storming Heaven: Class Composition and Struggle in Italian Autonomist Marxism*, 2nd ed. (London: Pluto Press, 2017); Martin Birkner and Robert Foltin, *(Post-)Operaismus. Von der Arbeiterautonomie zur Multitude* (Stuttgart: Schmetterling-Verlag, 2010).
35. Karl Marx, *Capital: Critique of Political Economy*, MECW, vol. 35, 379.
36. Kendra Coulter, "Horse Power: Gender, Work, and Wealth

in Canadian Show Jumping," in *Gender and Equestrian Sport: Riding around the World*, ed. Miriam Adelman and Jorge Knijnik (Dordrecht: Springer, 2013), 165–81, 171.

37. Such a horse is also unsuited to be ridden by optimization-mad managers; it is much more predestined to declare war on empires. Crazy Horse was the name of the Indigenous leader who dealt the US Army one of its most devastating defeats at the Battle of the Little Bighorn in 1876.

38. Shukin, *Animal Capital*, 88. For a stimulating analysis of Gramsci's text that sets it in relation it to post-Fordist phenomena like sexual freedom of movement and mad cow disease, see Frigga Haug, "Gramsci und die Produktion des Begehrens," *Psychologie und Gesellschaftskritik* 22 (1998), 75–92.

39. JK Gibson-Graham, *The End of Capitalism (As We Knew It): A Feminist Critique of Political Economy* (Oxford, UK / Cambridge, USA: Blackwell Publishers, 1996).

40. Marx, "Letters from the Deutsch-Französischen Jahrbücher," 144.

41. Cf. the influential text of Gayatri Chakravorty Spivak, "Can the Subaltern Speak?," in *Colonial Discourse and Post-colonial Theory: A Reader*, ed. Patrick Williams and Laura Chrisman (New York: Harvester / Wheatsheaf, 1994 [1988]), 66–111.

42. Dipesh Chakrabarty, *Provincializing Europe: Postcolonial thought and Historical Difference* (Princeton: Princeton University Press, 2000).

43. For a critical view on this, see Rutvica Andrijasevic, "The Spectacle of Misery: Gender, Migration and Representation

in Anti-trafficking Campaigns," *Feminist Review* 86 (2007), 24–44, as well as Sabine Hess, *Globalisierte Hausarbeit. Au-pair als Migrationsstrategie von Frauen aus Osteuropa* (Wiesbaden: VS Verlag, 2009).

44. Cf. Etienne Balibar and Sandro Mezzadra, "Borders, Citizenship, War, Class: A Discussion with Etienne Balibar and Sandro Mezzadra," *New Formations* 58 (2006), 10–30; Manuela Bojadžijev and Serhat Karakayali, "Autonomie der Migration. 10 Thesen zu einer Methode," in *Turbulente Ränder. Neue Perspektiven auf Migration an den Grenzen Europas*, ed. TRANSIT MIGRATION Forschungsgruppe (Bielefeld: Transcript, 2006), 203–209; Manuela Bojadžijev, *Die windige Internationale. Rassismus und Kämpfe der Migration* (Münster: Westfälisches Dampfboot, 2008).

45. Dimitris Papadopoulos and Vassilis Tsianos: "The Autonomy of Migration: The Animals of Undocumented Mobility," in *Deleuzian Encounters: Studies in Contemporary Social Issues*, ed. Anna Hickey-Moody and Peta Malins (Basingstoke: Palgrave Macmillan, 2007), 225.

46. Dimitris Papadopoulos, Niamh Stephenson, and Vassilis Tsianos, *Escape Routes: Control and Subversion in the 21st Century* (London: Pluto Press, 2008), 21.

47. William J. Broadnov, "Paradise Lost: Biosphere Retooled as Atmospheric Nightmare," *New York Times*, November 19, 1996.

UNDERGROUND ECOLOGIES

1. S. Markman, S. Leitner, C. Catchpole, S. Barnsley, C.T.

Müller, et al., "Pollutants Increase Song Complexity and the Volume of the Brain Area HVC in a Songbird," *PLoS ONE* 3,2 (2008), e1674, 1–6.
2. Errol Fuller, *The Passenger Pigeon* (Princeton: Princeton University Press, 2014), 9.
3. Ivan Akimushkin, *Sledy nevidannyx zverei* [The Tracks of Unseen Beasts] (Moscow: Geografgiz, 1961), cit. in Oxana Timofeeva, *Unconscious Desire for Communism*, manuscript, 2018.
4. Cited in Mark Payne, *The Animal Part: Human and Other Animals in the Poetic Imagination* (London/Chicago: University of Chicago Press, 2010), 71.
5. Eric Miller, "A Defect in Nature: The Figure of the Passenger Pigeon in Graeme Gibson and Other North American Writers" in *Restoring the Mystery of the Rainbow*, ed. V. Tinkler-Villani and C.C. Barfoot (Amsterdam / New York: Rodopi, 2011), 333–54, 353.
6. On account of the more than 1,000 taxidermically preserved specimens, in museums the passenger pigeon is the most frequently represented species of animal gone extinct in historical times. Cf. Dieter Luther, *Die ausgestorbenen Vögel der Welt*, Die Neue Brehm-Bücherei (Wittenberg: A. Ziemsen Verlag, 1986), 92–94.
7. David Garber, "Ben Klock: 'Ich bin kein Technopurist,'" *Vice Online*, October 21, 2015, https://thump.vice.com/de.
8. Paul B. Preciado, *Testo Junkie*, tr. Bruce Benderson (New York: The Feminist Press, 2013).
9. Paul B. Preciado, "Pharmaco-pornographic Politics:

Towards a New Gender Ecology," *Parallax* 14 (2008), 105–117, 108.
10. Preciado, *Testo Junkie*, 41.
11. For an inspiring reading of love and "animal queer," see Carmen Dell'Aversano, "The Love Whose Name Cannot Be Spoken: Queering the Human–Animal Bond," *Journal for Critical Animal Studies* 8, 1/2 (2010), 73–125.
12. William von Hippel and Frank A. von Hippel, "Sex Drugs and Animal Parts: Will Viagra Save Threatened Species?," *Environmental Conservation* 29,3 (2002), 277–81.
13. The belief in the effectiveness of exclusive medicines is not at all limited to Asia: according to *Forbes Magazine*, an extract from reindeer antlers is enjoying increasing popularity among US competitive athletes, because it promises to promote muscle growth and slow aging, to improve performance and regeneration after injuries—and of course, to boost your libido. Although no medical proof of these advertised effects has been found, trade in the miracle drug has proved a tidy business for the companies involved. David DiSalvo, "How to Squeeze Snake Oil from Deer Antlers and Make Millions," *Forbes Magazine*, October 11, 2013.
14. William von Hippel, Frank A. von Hippel, Norman Chan, and Clara Cheng, "Exploring the Use of Viagra in Place of Animal and Plant Potency Products in Traditional Chinese Medicine," *Environmental Conservation* 32,3 (2005), 235–38.
15. Craig Hoover, "Response to 'Sex, Drugs and Animal Parts: Will Viagra Save Threatened Species?,'" *Environmental Conservation* 30,4 (2003), 317–18; William von Hippel, "Is

Viagra a Viable Conservation Tool? Response to Hoover, 2003," *Environmental Conservation* 31,1 (2004), 4–6; Richard Damania and Erwin H. Bulte, "The Economics of Wildlife Farming and Endangered Species Conservation," *Ecological Economics* 62,3–4 (2007), 461–72.
16. Introduction, Nature Calendar 1991, Rocky Mountain Arsenal.
17. Cited in Alexander Wilson, *The Culture of Nature: North American Landscape from Disney to the Exxon* Valdez (Cambridge, MA: Blackwell, 1992), 281.
18. Mike Lee, "Military, Conservationists Unite to Deflect Urban Encroachment," *San Diego Union-Tribune*, July 26, 2005, cited in Peter Coates, Tim Cole, Marianna Dudley, and Chris Pearson, "Defending Nation, Defending Nature? Militarized Landscapes and Military Environmentalism in Britain, France, and the United States," *Environmental History* 16 (July 2011), 456–91, 490, n97.
19. Jeffrey P. Cohn, "A Makeover for Rocky Mountain Arsenal: Transforming a Superfund Site into a National Wildlife Refuge," *BIOSCIENCE* 49,4 (1999), 273–77, 274f.
20. Rachael E. Salcido, "The Rocky Mountain Arsenal National Wildlife Refuge: On a Rocky Road to Creating a Community Asset," *John Marshall Law Review* 47,4 (2014), 1399–430, 1404f.
21. Edmund Russell, *War and Nature: Fighting Humans and Insects with Chemicals from World War I to Silent Spring* (Cambridge MA: Cambridge University Press, 2001), 234f.
22. Eric Wagner, "The DMZ's Thriving Resident: The Crane," *Smithsonian Magazine*, April 2011.

23. Peter Coates, "From Hazard to Habitat (or Hazardous Habitat): The Lively and Lethal Afterlife of Rocky Flats, Colorado," *Progress in Physical Geography* 38,3 (2014), 286–300.
24. Julia Kristeva, *Powers of Horror: An Essay on Abjection* (New York: Columbia University Press, 1982).
25. Timothy Morton, *Ecology without Nature: Rethinking Environmental Aesthetics* (Cambridge, MA: Harvard University Press, 2007), 159f.
26. Morton, *Ecology without Nature*.
27. William Cronon, ed., *Uncommon Ground: Rethinking the Human Place in Nature* (New York: W.W. Norton & Co, 1996), 28.
28. Thomas A. Sebeok, *Communication Measures to Bridge Ten Millennia* (BMI/ONWI-532, prepared by Research Center for Language and Semiotic Studies, Indiana University, for Office of Nuclear Waste Isolation, Battelle Memorial Institute, Columbus, OH, 1984).
29. Sebeok, *Communication Measures to Bridge Ten Millennia*, 24.
30. Sebeok, *Communication Measures to Bridge Ten Millennia*, 24.
31. Sebeok, *Communication Measures to Bridge Ten Millennia*, 24.
32. Cecil C. Konijnendijk, *The Forest and the City: The Cultural Landscape of Urban Woodland* (Berlin: Springer, 2008), 111.
33. Countless films of this genre in the postwar period presented Austrian nature as an idyllic world in bright, kitschy colours. Particular stress was placed on a symbolic Alpine landscape as the home of order, security, family, and religion. In the pure *Heimatfilm* the Austrian national consciousness, bruised by decades of defeat and

defamation, enjoyed a soothing vacation from its messy history. At least the hero of the *Heimatfilm*, as a son of the mountains, always did everything right. In the seemingly harmless *Heimatfilm*, homeland (*Heimat*) is always the mountain and the landscape.

34. William Cronon, "The Trouble with Wilderness; or, Getting Back to the Wrong Nature," in *Uncommon Ground*, 69–90, 73.
35. Cronon, "The Trouble with Wilderness," 75.
36. Cronon, "The Trouble with Wilderness," 87.
37. Juan José Katira Ramirez, personal conversation with the author, *The School of the Jaguar*, curated by dancer and choreographer Amanda Piña, deSingel, Antwerp, Belgium, December 8, 2017.
38. For example, Pakhtuns, historically known as Afghans, are considered to be the world's largest tribal society. In contrast to many other tribal societies in the world, the Pakhtuns have never been conquered. The successful resistance of the Pakhtun tribes against Western and Eastern attempts at subjugating them in the twentieth and twenty-first centuries leaves little room in the "cemetery of the great powers" for the Western will to victimize.
39. Johannes Neurath, *Peyote, Politik und Polyontologien*, lecture, University of Art and Design Linz, June 6, 2018.
40. Monserrat Suàrez-Rodríguez, Isabel Lopez-Rull, and Constantino Macías Garcia, "Incorporation of Cigarette Butts into Nests Reduces Nest Ectoparasite Load in Urban Birds: New Ingredients for an Old Recipe?," *Biology Letters* 9,1 (2012), 1–3.

41. Martin Vieweg, "Kurios: Nester aus Kippen," *wissenschaft.de*, December 5, 2012.

CLOUDY SWORDS

1. Paul F. Russell, *Man's Mastery of Malaria* (Oxford: Oxford University Press, 1955), 244, citing David Turnbull, *Masons, Tricksters, and Cartographers: Comparative Studies in the Sociology of Scientific and Indigenous Knowledge* (New York: Routledge, 2000), 182n13.
2. Mary Kosut and Lisa Jean Moore, "Urban Api-Ethnography: The Matter of Relations between Humans and Honeybees," in *Mattering: Feminism, Science, and Materialism*, ed. Victoria Pitts-Taylor (New York/London: New York University Press, 2016), 245–57, 246.
3. Kosut and Moore, "Urban Api-Ethnography," 246. Hegemonic images are always unstable. Although even the behaviour of bees is predictable, it is not completely so, as the case of so-called Africanized killer bees shows: escaped from a Brazilian breeding experiment in 1957, which had crossed the European honeybee with African honeybees, many feral swarms developed, ultimately crossing the US border in 1990, where, because of their "mobility and aggressiveness" as well as their "unwillingness to settle into working class stability," they were considered "threats to the order and efficiency of production." Anna L. Tsing, "Empowering Nature, or: Some Gleanings in Bee Culture," in *Naturalizing Power: Essays in Feminist Cultural Analysis*,

ed. S. Yanagisako and C. Delaney (New York: Routledge, 1995), 113–43, 135.
4. Cf. Juan Antonio Ramírez, *The Beehive Metaphor: From Gaudí to Le Corbusier* (London: Reaktion, 2000), 25–35.
5. Tammy Horn, *Bees in America: How the Honey Bee Shaped a Nation* (University of Kentucky Press, 2006), 19–64.
6. Jens Martin Gurr, "The Mass-Slaughter of Native Americans in Jim Jarmusch's *Dead Man:* A Complex Interplay of Word and Image," in *Word & Image in Colonial and Postcolonial Literatures and Cultures*, ed. Michael Meyer, Gesellschaft für die Neuen Englischsprachigen Literaturen (Amsterdam: Brill Academic Publishers, 2009), 354–71, 355.
7. The use of biological weapons, like bees and other insects, is neither exclusive to the US nor anything really new; see Jeffery Lockwood, *Six-Legged Soldiers: Using Insects as Weapons of War* (Oxford: Oxford University Press, 2008).
8. Jake Kosek, "Ecologies of the Empire: On the New Uses of the Honeybee," *Cultural Anthropology* 25,4 (2010), 650–78, 656.
9. Jake Kosek, "New Uses of the Honeybee," in *Global Political Ecology*, ed. Richard Peet, Paul Robbins, and Michael Watts (London: Routledge, 2011), 227–51
10. Lisa Jean Moore and Mary Kosut, *Buzz: Urban Beekeeping and the Power of the Bee* (New York/London: New York University Press, 2013), 138.
11. Jay Bybee, "Memorandum for John Rizzo, Acting General Counsel of the Central Intelligence Agency," U.S. Department of Justice, Office of Legal Counsel, August 1, 2009, 1–18, 2, www.hsdl.org.
12. Bybee, "Memorandum for John Rizzo," 3.

13. Cf. Neel Ahuja, "Abu Zubaydah and the Caterpillar," *Social Text* 29,1 (2011), 127–49, 128.
14. Ahuja, "Abu Zubaydah and the Caterpillar," 129.
15. Ahuja, "Abu Zubaydah and the Caterpillar," 134.
16. Ahuja, "Abu Zubaydah and the Caterpillar," 133. See also Jasbir K. Puar and Amit S. Rai, "Monster, Terrorist, Fag: The War on Terrorism and the Production of Docile Patriots," *Social Text* 72 (2002), 117–48.
17. John Robert McNeill, *Mosquito Empires: Ecology and War in the Greater Caribbean, 1620–1914* (Cambridge, MA: Cambridge University Press, 2010).
18. Diane M. Nelson, "A Social Science Fiction of Fevers, Delirium, and Discovery: The Calcutta Chromosome, the Colonial Laboratory, and the Postcolonial New Human," *Science Fiction Studies* 30,2 (2003), 246–66, 260.
19. Nelson, "A Social Science Fiction," 260f.
20. Bruno Latour, *The Pasteurization of France* (Cambridge, MA: Harvard University Press, 1988), 141.
21. Nelson, "A Social Science Fiction," 247.
22. Jeanne Guillemin: "Choosing Scientific Patrimony: Sir Ronald Ross, Alphonse Laveran, and the Mosquito-Vector Hypothesis for Malaria," *Journal of the History of Medicine and Allied Sciences* 57,4 (2002), 385–409.
23. Margaret Lock and Vinh-Kim Nguyen, *An Anthropology of Biomedicine* (Hoboken, NJ: Wiley-Blackwell, 2010), 179.
24. Lock and Vinh-Kim Nguyen, *Anthropology of Biomedicine*, 43f. William B. Cohen sees this critically, at least with regard to French expansion politics. According to Cohen, it was not so much medical knowledge from tropical

medicine, which soldiers in battle were often skeptical of, and whose prescriptions, like the taking of quinine, were often only half-heartedly followed, but rather, contrariwise, the political and social stabilization of French colonial areas that made possible the increased recruiting of local troops and the construction of mosquito-unfriendly military architecture (buildings made of clay, brick, and stone, instead of tents), which in turn at first led to lower losses due to malaria. (William B. Cohen, "Malaria and French Imperialism," *Journal of African History* 24 (1983), 23–36.)
25. Emma Umana Clasberry, *Culture of Names in Africa: A Search for Cultural Identity* (New York: Xlibris Corp, 2012), 54.
26. Clasberry, *Culture of Names in Africa*. See also Helen Callaway, *Gender, Culture and Empire: European Women in Colonial Nigeria* (Basingstoke: Macmillan, 1987), 65ff.
27. Ambe J. Njoh points to the aspect of ideological division, since the segregated part of the local population was ascribed the status of "health threat," while to the other part, who as servants were allowed to live in the healthy, European zones, this could appear as personal gratification and inclusive appreciation. Cf. Ambe J. Njoh, "Urban Planning as a Tool of Power and Social Control in Colonial Africa," *Planning Perspectives* 24,3 (2009), 301–317, 303.
28. Philip D. Curtin, "Medical Knowledge and Urban Planning in Tropical Africa," *American Historical Review* 90,3 (1985), 594–613, 602.
29. Jonathan Roberts, "*Korle and the Mosquito:* Histories and

Memories of the Antimalaria Campaign, Accra, 1942–45," *Journal of African History* 51 (2010), 343–365, 348.
30. Roberts explains: "Though there is no record of outright resistance by the migrant workers hired as human bait, it appears that they took measures to preserve their dignity, and, especially, to avoid mosquito bites." (*"Korle and the Mosquito,"* 358.)
31. Roberts, *"Korle and the Mosquito,"* 355.
32. Harriet Deacon, "Racial Segregation and Medical Discourse in Nineteenth-Century Cape Town," *Journal of Southern African Studies* 22,2 (1996), 287–308.
33. Carl H. Nightingale, *Segregation: A Global History of Divided Cities* (Chicago: University of Chicago Press, 2015), 176.
34. Cf. Curtin, "Medical Knowledge and Urban Planning in Tropical Africa"; Njoh, "Urban Planning as a Tool of Power and Social Control in Colonial Africa."
35. Cited in John W. Cell, "Anglo-Indian Medical Theory and the Origins of Segregation in West Africa," *American Historical Review* 91,2 (1986), 307–335, 308.
36. Cell, "Anglo-Indian Medical Theory and the Origins of Segregation," 332.
37. Cf. Paul S. Sutter, "Nature's Agents or Agents of Empire? Entomological Workers and Environmental Change During the Construction of the Panama Canal," *Isis* 98,4 (2007), 724–54; Maria Kaika, "Dams as Symbols of Modernization: The Urbanization of Nature Between Geographical Imagination and Materiality," *Annals of the Association of American Geographers* 96,2 (2006), 276–301.
38. Sutter, "Nature's Agents or Agents of Empire?," 725.

39. Mitchell, *Rule of Experts*, 19–53, 26.
40. At that time, the Rockefeller Sanitary Commission for the Eradication of Hookworm Disease had just finished its successful campaign against a hookworm species called *Necator americanus* (Latin for "American killer") in eleven southern American states, which lasted from 1909 to 1915, and became part of the Rockefeller Foundation International Health Division. The connection between poverty, race, and infections by the murderous hookworm played an important role in the formation of cultural perception and self-image of those affected. Cf Matt Wray, *Not Quite White: White Trash and the Boundaries of Whiteness* (Durham: Duke University Press, 2006), 96–132.
41. Wray, *Not Quite White*, 96.
42. Ricardo Salvatore, "Imperial Mechanics: South America's Hemispheric Integration in the Machine Age," *American Quarterly* 58,3 (2006), 663–91, 663f.
43. Neel Ahuja, *Bioinsecurities: Disease Interventions, Empire, and the Government of Species* (Durham: Duke University Press, 2016), 19.
44. Ahuja, *Bioinsecurities*, 77.
45. Ahuja, *Bioinsecurities*, 73. For a discussion of the US Army's cinematic warfare against the anopheles mosquito in the 1940s, which was here portrayed as the second main war enemy and turned into a "placeholder for warnings about alcoholism, homosexuality, loose morals, sexually transmitted diseases and the fear (or desire) of sexual penetration," see Gudrun Löhner, "Anopheles Anni vs. Malaria Mike," in *Tiere im Film. Eine Menschheitsgeschichte*

der Moderne, ed. Maren Möhring, Massimo Perinelli, and Olaf Stieglitz (Köln: Böhlau, 2009), 193–205, 194.

46. Ahuja, *Bioinsecurities*, 99; see also 216n13.
47. Federico Caprotti, "Malaria and Technological Networks: Medical Geography in the Pontine Marshes, Italy, in the 1930s," *Geographical Journal* 172,2 (2006), 145–55, 147.
48. Caprotti, "Malaria and Technological Networks," 149f.
49. Caprotti, "Malaria and Technological Networks." 153.
50. Leo Barney Slater and Margaret Humphreys, "Parasites and Progress: Ethical Decision-Making and the Santee-Cooper Malaria Study, 1944–1949," *Perspectives in Biology and Medicine* 51,1 (2008), 103–120, 107.
51. Nicolas Rasmussen, "Plant Hormones in War and Peace: Science, Industry, and Government in the Development of Herbicides in 1940s America," *Isis* 92,2 (2001), 291–316, 292.
52. Eric D. Carter, "'God Bless General Perón': DDT and the Endgame of Malaria Eradication in Argentina in the 1940s," *Journal of the History of Medicine and Allied Sciences* 64,1 (2008), 78–122.
53. Mitchell, *Rule of Experts*, 50.
54. Sunil S. Amrith, *Decolonizing International Health: India and Southeast Asia, 1930–65* (New York: Palgrave Macmillan, 2006), 104.
55. Alfons Labisch, "Species Sanitation of Malaria in the Netherlands East Indies (1913–1942): An Example of Applied Medical History?," *Michael Quarterly* 7 (2010), 296–306, 298.
56. David Turnbull, *Masons, Tricksters, and Cartographers:*

Comparative Studies in the Sociology of Scientific and Indigenous Knowledge (New York: Routledge, 2000), 165–94, 166.
57. Turnbull, *Masons, Tricksters, and Cartographers*, 168.
58. Catherine Lutz and Jon Elliston, "Domestic Terror," *The Nation*, October 14, 2002, 14–16.
59. Nelson, "A Social Science Fiction," 263n6.
60. Uli Beisel and Christophe Boëte, "The Flying Public Health Tool: Genetically Modified Mosquitoes and Malaria Control," *Science as Culture* 22,1 (2013), 38–60, 58. This is a bioeconomic cake that emerging markets like Brazil also want a piece of Cf. Luisa Reis-Castro and Kim Hendrickx, "Winged Promises: Exploring the Discourse on Transgenic Mosquitoes in Brazil," *Technology in Society* 35 (2013), 118–28.
61. Uli Beisel, "Markets and Mutations: Mosquito Nets and the Politics of Disentanglement in Global Health," *Geoforum* 66 (2016), 145–55, 145.
62. Beisel, "Markets and Mutations," 150.
63. Beisel, "Markets and Mutations," 153.
64. Eva Johach, "Termitewerden: Staatenbildende Insekten im Industriezeitalter," *Kultur & Gespenster* 4 (2007), 20–37, 21. Cf. Douglas Starr and Felix Driver, "Imagining the Tropical Colony: Henry Smeathman and the Termites of Sierra Leone," in *Tropical Visions in an Age of Empire*, ed. Felix Driver and Luciana Martins (Chicago: University of Chicago Press, 2005), 92–112.
65. It was long assumed that it was *Reticulitermes flavipes* (*Kollar*), the most widespread termite of North America. Current research suggests another conclusion: the

Hamburg termite population seems to consist of the southern European "cousins": *Reticulitermes lucifugus*. See Udo Sellenschlo, *Vorratsschädlinge und Hausungeziefer: Bestimmungstabellen für Mitteleuropa* (Heidelberg: Springer Verlag, 2010), 49.

66. Nel Yomtov, *From Termite Den to Office Building* (Ann Arbor: Cherry Lake Publishing, 2014), 10.
67. According to Abraham Margolis, the chief engineer of the enterprise, the driving force for the project was the high cost of fuel after World War I. But Margolis himself saw much more in electrical heating: social-political, hygienic, medical, and ecological aspects. After he was driven out of the corporation's management by the National Socialists in the 1930s, Margolis settled in the United Kingdom and continued his work with another company, which would bring district heating to Pimlico, a London residential area. (Wolfgang Mock, "Margolis, Abraham," *Neue Deutsche Biographie* 16, 1990, 169f. Cf. Charlotte Johnson, "District Heating as Heterotopia: Tracing the Social Contract through Domestic Energy Infrastructure in Pimlico," *Economic Anthropology* 3,1 (2016), 94–105.)
68. "Karoviertel, Termiten-Attacke," *Hamburger Morgenpost*, February 9, 2009.
69. According to expert interviews with various municipal officials in April and May 2013 (together with the architect and researcher Christina Linorter).
70. Thermidor was the eleventh month of the French revolutionary calendar, which lasted from the middle of July to the middle of August and literally means "the

month of heat." Maximilien de Robespierre was toppled in this month of the year 1794.

71. www.termidorhome.com
72. According to expert interviews with various municipal officials in April and May 2013 (together with Christina Linorter).
73. Silke Klöver, *Was hat die Globalisierung mit uns zu tun? Grundwissen erwerben—Zusammenhänge erkennen* (Buxtehude: Persen Verlag, 2011), 21.
74. Theodore A. Evans, Brian T. Forschler, and Grace J. Kenneth, "Biology of Invasive Termites: A Worldwide Review," *Annual Review Entomology* 58 (2012), 455–74, 457.
75. Theodore A. Evans, "Invasive Termites," in *Biology of Termites: A Modern Synthesis*, ed. David Edward Bignell, Yves Roisin, and Nathan Lo (New York: Springer, 2011), 519–62, 520.
76. Evans, "Invasive Termites," 521.
77. Donna Haraway, "The Biopolitics of Postmodern Bodies: 'Constitutions of Self in Immune System Discourse," in *Simians, Cyborgs, and Women: The Reinvention of Nature* (New York: Routledge, 1991), 203–230.
78. The paragraph from the chapter "The Planet without a Visa" in Trotsky's autobiography, *My Life*, reminds us (living in the times of whistleblower Edward Snowden and Sci-Hub founder Alexandra Elbakyan) of the continuities between his and our epoch: "I must admit that the roll-call of the western European democracies on the question of the right of asylum has given me, aside from other things, more than a few merry minutes. At times, it seemed as

if I were attending a 'pan-European' performance of a one-act comedy on the theme of principles of democracy. Its text might have been written by Bernard Shaw if the Fabian fluid that runs in his veins had been strengthened by even so much as five per cent of Jonathan Swift's blood. But whoever may have written the text, the play remains very instructive: *Europe without a Visa*. There is no need to mention America. The United States is not only the strongest, but also the most terrified country. Hoover recently explained his passion for fishing by pointing out the democratic nature of this pastime. If this be so—although I doubt it—it is at all events one of the few survivals of democracy still existing in the United States. There the right of asylum has been absent for a long time. *Europe and America without a visa*. But these two continents own the other three. This means—*The planet without a visa*." Leon Trotsky, *My Life* (New York: Grosset & Dunlap, 1960 [1930]), 579.

79. Hugh Raffles, *Insectopedia* (New York: Pantheon, 2010), 469–73.
80. Mitchell, *Rule of Experts*.
81. Clapperton Changanetsa Mavhunga, *The Mobile Workshop: Mobility, Technology, and Human-Animal Interaction in Gonarezhou (National Park), 1850–Present*, dissertation, University of Michigan, 2008, 7.
82. Bambule was the name of a countercultural trailer park of squatters in the aforesaid Karovierterl, where the Hamburg termites also live. Massive protests against the police clearing of the alternative living project became the subject

of international press coverage. While *Bambule machen* (making bambule) is a northern German slang expression for rioting and rampaging, *bamboula* goes back to the name for a big drum and the dance that accompanied this drum—both had their origin in Africa and were brought to the US through the "traffic in human flesh." Particularly after the Haitian revolution, slaves gathered in Congo Square on the edge of the French Quarter in New Orleans to dance the bamboula.

83. Wilhelm Bölsche, "Der Termitenstaat. Schilderung eines geheimnisvollen Volkes (1931)," 52, cited in Johach, "Termitewerden," 31.
84. Bölsche, "Der Termitenstaat," 34.
85. Karl Escherich, inaugural speech at Ludwig Maximilian University in Munich on November 25, 1933.
86. Jean L. Sutherland, "Protozoa from Australian Termites," *Quarterly Journal of Microscopical Science* 2 (1933), 145–73, 76.
87. Donna J. Haraway, "Otherworldly Conversations; Terran Topics; Local Terms," *Science as Culture* 3,1 (1992), 94.
88. Myra Hird, *Sex, Gender and Science* (Houndmills: Palgrave Macmillan, 2004), 68.
89. Nikki Sullivan, "The Somatechnics of Perception and the Matter of the Non/human: A Critical Response to the New Materialism," *European Journal of Women's Studies* 19 (2012), 299–313, 306.
90. *Das purpurne Muttermal*, program (Wien: Burgtheater/Akademietheater Wien, 2006).
91. Rupert D.V. Glasgow, *The Minimal Self* (Würzburg: Würzburg University Press, 2017), 358n860.

BLACK HOLE SUN

1. What strikes capable members of the middle class as plausible is easily seen through by others. A French study showed that exactly those people who cannot maintain gainful employment because of their age or a shortage of jobs, or out of mental or physical infirmity, are clearly in favour of state regulation of animal husbandry. They know from their own experience that state-guaranteed rights offer much more security than relying on the goodwill of farmers and the individual benevolent decisions of others.
2. Fabian Federl, "Veganer und Drogen. Hört erst mal auf zu koksen!," *Der Tagesspiegel*, December 24, 2015.
3. This is a translation of the title used in the German version of the article: Mike Pearl, "So unmoralisch ist es, Kokain zu nehmen," *Vice Magazine*, May 28, 2016, www.vice.com/de. The original in English: "How Unethical Is Buying Cocaine," May 23, 2016, www.vice.com.
4. Cited in "Bio-Essen kaufen, aber Kokain nehmen? Polizeichefin kritisiert scheinheilige Mittelschichtler," *Der Stern*, August 1, 2018. Cf. Lizze Dearden, "Violent Crime 'Stabilising in London,' Police Say after 87 People Killed So Far in 2018," *The Independent*, August 1, 2018, www.independent.co.uk. For a more serious discussion of the phenomenon of increasing gang violence in London, see Jo Cardwell, Claire Dissington, and Brian Richardson, "Out of Control? Youth Crime, Class and Capitalism," *International Socialism* 159 (July 2018), http://isj.org.uk.
5. Cited in Donna Haraway, "Situated Knowledges: The

Science Question in Feminism and the Privilege of Partial Perspective," *Feminist Studies* 14,3 (1988), 575–99, 596n1.
6. Theodor W. Adorno, *Minima Moralia: Reflections from Damaged Life*, tr. E.F.M. Jephcott (New York: Verso, 2005), 57.
7. Friedrich Nietzsche, *Thus Spoke Zarathustra*, ed. Adrian del Caro and Robert Pippin, tr. Adrian del Caro (Cambridge: Cambridge University Press, 2006), 184.
8. Ernst Bloch, "Etwas fehlt . . . über die Widersprüche der Utopischen Sehnsucht" (Something Is Missing . . . about the Contradictions of Utopian Longing), radio interview with Theodor W. Adorno (1964); *Tendenz—Latenz—Utopie*, Ergänzungsband zur Gesamtausgabe (Frankfurt a. M.: Suhrkamp, 1978), 350–68.
9. Max Brod, *Über Franz Kafka* (Frankfurt a. M.: Fischer Taschenbuch Verlag, 1974), 70.
10. Peter Stine, "Franz Kafka and Animals," *Contemporary Literature* 22,1 (1981), 58–80, 70; Eric Williams, "Of Cinema, Food, and Desire: Franz Kafka's 'Investigations of a Dog,'" *College Literature* 34,4 (2007), 92–124, 116f. and 119n13; Jens Hanssen, "Kafka and Arabs," *Critical Inquiry* 39,1 (2012), 167–97, 180f. On the human-animal relationship in Kafka, see also Christina Gerhardt, "The Ethics of Animals in Adorno and Kafka," *New German Critique* 97,33:1 (2006), 159–78; Chris Danta, "Kafka's Mousetrap: The Fable of the Dying Voice," *SubStance* 117,37:3 (2008), 152–68; Marc Much and Donna Yard, eds., *Kafka's Creatures. Animals, Hybrids, and Other Fantastic Beings* (Lanham: Lexington Books, 2010).

11. John Varley, *The Persistence of Vision* (New York: The Dial Press/James Wade, 1978).
12. Varley, *The Persistence of Vision*, 6.
13. See Eva Hayward, "Fingery Eyes: Impressions of Cup Corals," *Cultural Anthropology* 25,4 (2010), 577–99. For feminist-inspired rearticulations and interrogations of touch as a world-generating relative of the visual, see Lorraine Code, *What Can She Know?: Feminist Theory and the Construction of Knowledge* (Ithaca: Cornell University Press, 1991).
14. Timothy Morton, *Humankind: Solidarity with Nonhuman People* (London/New York: Verso, 2017), 144.
15. Morton, *Humankind*, 163.
16. Morton, *Humankind*, 144.
17. Morton, *Humankind*, 179.
18. Today's *crip theory* is a critical cultural that has "been deployed to resist the contemporary spectacle of able-bodied heteronormativity." Robert McCruer, *Crip Theory: Cultural Signs of Queerness and Disability* (New York: NYU Press, 2006), 3.
19. Marion von Osten and Peter Spillmann, *Be Creative!—Der kreative Imperativ* (Zürich: Museum für Gestaltung Zürich, 2002).

GEOFFREY C. HOWES has translated books by Peter Rosei, Robert Musil, Jürg Laederach, and Gabriele Petricek, as well as stories, essays, and poems by more than thirty authors.

CORVIN RUSSELL is an activist, writer, and translator based in Toronto. His current focus is Indigenous solidarity and environmental justice work.

FAHIM AMIR is a Viennese philosopher and author. He has taught at various universities and art academies in Europe and Latin America. His research explores the thresholds of natures, cultures, and urbanism; art and utopia; and colonial historicity and modernism.